Rory's Club is the story of Holywood Golf Club's passion for the game of golf and of its most outstanding member, whose roots remain at the club's very heart.

RORY'S CLUB

Foreword by Rory McIlroy

edited by
Claude Costecalde
Christina Captieux

HOLYWOOD GOLF CLUB

BOOKLINK

Rory looks at a shot during the par-three contest prior to the start of the 2013 Masters Tournament at Augusta National Golf Club, Georgia on 10 April 2013.
ANDREW REDINGTON/GETTY IMAGES

Nick taught me to take the shot you know you can make, not the one you hope to.

Rory poses with Nick Faldo after winning the Under 17 Division of the 2006 Faldo Junior Series during day two of the Faldo Junior Series Final at The Celtic Manor Resort on October 6, 2006 in Newport, Wales.
RICHARD HEATHCOTE/GETTY IMAGES

Rory McIlroy's journey is a superb example of how a dedicated young player can achieve great success. *Rory's Club* **is a great tribute to his formative years, his relationship with Holywood Golf Club, and the golfing fraternity he has forged – not just in Northern Ireland but with players around the world.**

As he was growing up, Rory was lucky enough to be mentored by some of the most experienced players in the game, like Darren Clarke OBE and Sir Nick Faldo.

Nick first met Rory when he won **The Faldo Series** under-15s tournament in 2004. The Faldo Series was established as a charity in 1996 to provide opportunities for young golfers like Nick Dougherty and Yani Tseng. Rory is a former three-time winner of this global golf development programme. Thousands of participants take part every year in tournaments held in more than 25 different countries. Age category winners at each event qualify for either the Faldo Series Asia grand final at **Mission Hills Golf Club**, Shenzhen, China or the Faldo Series grand final, also hosted by Nick Faldo at the **Lough Erne Resort** in Enniskillen, Northern Ireland.

Rory supported Nick at the launch of the **Faldo Championship Course** at Lough Erne in 2010. He partnered up with his other close mentor Darren Clarke. Needless to say, the duo won the tournament. The luck of the Northern Irish... they have a gift for the game.

We hope you find time to enjoy *Rory's Club,* explore his homeland and discover the stories and people behind the remarkable career of one of our most promising young golfers.

Rory and Darren Clarke wait on the 3rd hole during the first round of the BMW PGA Championship at Wentworth Club on May 26, 2011 in Virginia Water, England.
DAVID CANNON/GETTY IMAGES

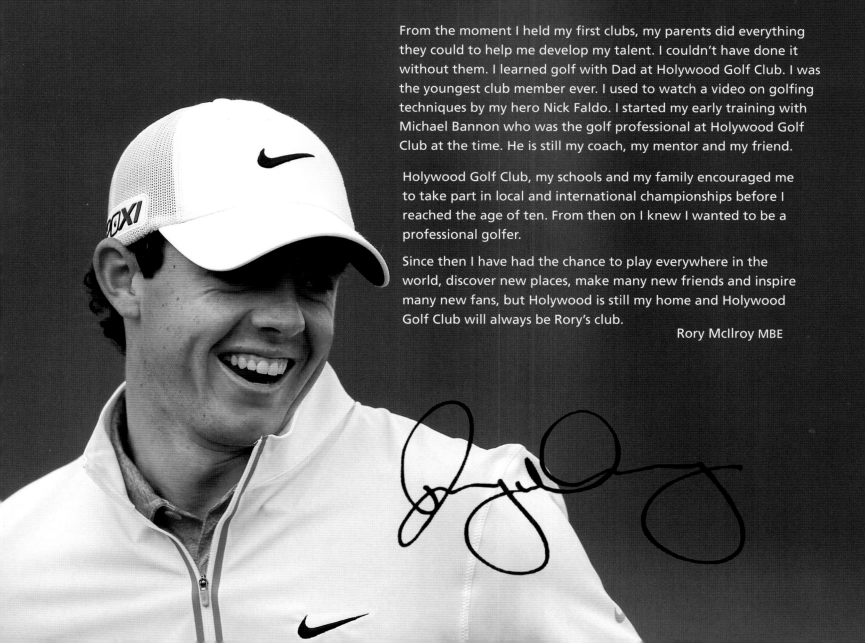

It all began in Holywood, my hometown. My roots are there, my family and first friends live there, it was where I went to school, and it was where I started playing golf.

From the moment I held my first clubs, my parents did everything they could to help me develop my talent. I couldn't have done it without them. I learned golf with Dad at Holywood Golf Club. I was the youngest club member ever. I used to watch a video on golfing techniques by my hero Nick Faldo. I started my early training with Michael Bannon who was the golf professional at Holywood Golf Club at the time. He is still my coach, my mentor and my friend.

Holywood Golf Club, my schools and my family encouraged me to take part in local and international championships before I reached the age of ten. From then on I knew I wanted to be a professional golfer.

Since then I have had the chance to play everywhere in the world, discover new places, make many new friends and inspire many new fans, but Holywood is still my home and Holywood Golf Club will always be Rory's club.

Rory McIlroy MBE

I used to play from 7.30 a.m. until 10 p.m. in the summer at Holywood Golf Club.
I have great memories playing with friends, family and Dad.
I played 54 holes a day.
It's just what I did.

PRIVATE FAMILY COLLECTION

Rory's Club is the story of Holywood Golf Club
and its champion's success.

It is a fascinating story exploring Rory McIlroy's golfing roots
here at the club and beyond – as an international champion who
is earning a special place in golfing history.

As a tiny toddler, Rory teetered across the club's fairways and
greens, following in the footsteps of his father Gerry and
grandfather Jimmy McIlroy, playing with clubs specially
shortened for his tiny frame. Rory definitely had golf in his blood
and bones.

His formative years of hard training under the watchful eye of his
father and the expert tutelage of top coach Michael Bannon stood
the young champion in good stead.

Nurtured at Holywood Golf Club, Rory has maintained a lifelong
and exciting association with the institution. Rory's love of the
game has inspired a new generation of golfers, bringing thousands
of young people to the sport.

PRIVATE FAMILY COLLECTION

Northern Ireland – Golf Capital of the World

In recent years, Northern Ireland has dominated the field, with top class players smashing records and winning tournaments around the world.

Irish Open, Royal Portrush Golf Club, Northern Ireland, 2012
PRESSEYE.COM

US Open champions Rory McIlroy and Graeme McDowell (winner 2010) with British Open champion Darren Clarke, pictured in Portrush on 19 July 2011.
DARREN KIDD/PRESSEYE.COM

In June 2010, Graeme McDowell, or G-Mac, as he is affectionately known, won the **US Open** at **Pebble Beach Resorts**, California, becoming the first Northern Irishman to do so and the first European US Open winner since Tony Jacklin in 1970. After his twentieth attempt in June 2011, Darren Clarke won his first major competition at the **Open Championship** at **Royal St George's Golf Club** in Sandwich, Kent at the tender age of 42. His victory made him the third major winner from Northern Ireland in only 13 months.

International Success

Like his fellow Northern Irish players, Rory's globetrotting career continues apace. With scores of record-breaking achievements under his belt, his eye is firmly set on milestones to come.

After winning the US **PGA Championship**, his second major championship, in South Carolina in August 2012 and being named PGA Player of the Year 2012, the future is looking very promising for Rory McIlroy MBE.

UNICEF Ireland

As an international sportsman, Rory has captured hearts and minds around the world. He has also moved beyond sporting boundaries and onto the international stage as UNICEF Ireland's goodwill ambassador for children (2011).

Rory was appointed a UNICEF Ireland ambassador in March 2011.
PRESSEYE.COM

Northern Ireland ... golf capital of the world!

This is what Rory tweeted in response to his pal Darren Clarke winning the British Open Championship in 2011. Northern Ireland has contributed more major champions in the modern era than any other European country, with three in the space of just 13 months from the US Open Championship in 2010 to the British Open Championship in 2011.

(Left–right) Graeme McDowell, Darren Clarke and Rory McIlroy of Northern Ireland pose together on the Black Course at Bethpage State Park, Farmingdale, New York, on 16 June 2009, during the second day of previews to the 109th US Open Championship.
ANDREW REDINGTON/GETTY IMAGES

With the success of Rory McIlroy, Darren Clarke and Graeme McDowell at major championships in recent years, Northern Ireland is no stranger to golfing success.

Notable golfers include Fred Daly (winner of the Open in 1947), Ryder Cup players Ronan Rafferty and David Feherty; and leading PGA European Tour professionals David Jones, Michael Hoey (a winner in 2011) and Gareth Maybin.

Northern Ireland has also contributed several players to the Great Britain and Ireland Walker Cup team – including Alan Dunbar and Paul Cutler, who played on the victorious 2011 side in Scotland.

Titanic Belfast – where Jimmy McIlroy, Rory's grandfather, worked on the Belfast shipyards. It is visible along the coast from Royal Belfast Golf Club, the oldest golf club in Ireland.
CHRISTOPHERHEANEY/TITANIC BELFAST

The Mourne Mountains – a stunning backdrop to the Royal County Down Golf Club
SCENIC IRELAND

County Fermanagh – the tenth hole on the Faldo
Championship Course at Lough Erne Resort in Enniskillen,
County Fermanagh (7,167 yards, par 72)

DAVID CANNON/GETTY IMAGES

St Patrick's Trail begins in Bangor, County Down, where Michael Bannon
ran a golf school. Darren Clarke's hometown, Dungannon, sits 12 miles
(19 kilometres) north of **Armagh** city (ABOVE).

SCENIC IRELAND

Graeme McDowell plays his second shot on the seventeenth hole during the first round of the 2012 Irish Open on 28 June 2012, on the Dunluce Links at Royal Portrush Golf Club.
DAVID CANNON/GETTY IMAGES

After studying engineering at Queen's University, Belfast, Graeme McDowell turned professional in 2002. He went on to win that season's **Volvo Scandinavian Masters** (2–5 August), which was only his fourth start of the European Tour. That win led to McDowell being given honorary life membership at the **Royal Portrush Golf Club**, which lies west of Northern Ireland's only UNESCO World Heritage Site, the spectacular Giant's Causeway.

The Giant's Causeway and scenic north coast – Graeme McDowell's Royal Portrush Golf Club lies 7 miles (11 kilometres) west of the causeway.
SCENIC IRELAND

Holywood is a small coastal town on Belfast Lough, just east of Belfast city in County Down.

Holywood's history dates back to the sixth century AD. When the Normans first landed, they named the area *Sanctus Boscus*, meaning 'of the holy wood', after the dense forest surrounding an old Irish monastery there.

I have so many great memories from Holywood.
I'm sure I'll gain many more over the years.
It's a really nice parkland course overlooking Belfast
Lough and the countryside. Rory

According to reliable local evidence, the first golf to be played in Northern Ireland was on a roughly marked-out course at Kinnegar on the shores of Belfast Lough, near Holywood. Golfers would frequently have played in trying conditions, buffeted by strong winds and rain sweeping in from the Irish Sea.

'Links' is a term used to describe golf courses located within four miles of the coast. Specifically, it refers to the type of soil and terrain on which they are built. Only 92 of the courses in Scotland (17 per cent) are true links courses, although this includes most of the historical courses. Another ten per cent are coastal, with some properties of links courses and moorland vegetation.

In 1881, the Belfast merchant Thomas Sinclair found himself playing golf at **St Andrews Links** in Fife, Scotland. Immediately smitten by the game, on his return home he sought out George L. Baillie, a local teacher and experienced golfer, originally from Musselburgh in Scotland. Together they approached the laird of Holywood, Captain John Harrison, who generously gave permission for a golf course to be laid out free of charge on his land at Kinnegar.

Holywood Golf Club Emerges

In 1892, the community's sporting society was left without a golf course when it relocated to Carnalea, west of Bangor, County Down. Local players decided to pool their resources, forming Holywood Golf Club in 1904.

The first nine-hole course was laid out on ground known as the 'Irish Hill', which was rented from Henry Harrison Esq. Harrison was elected the first president of the club and held office until 1924. The new course extended to the upper slope of the hill. In snowy weather the whole hill was always opened to the public for tobogganing.

Royal Belfast Golf Course, 1893
ROYAL BELFAST GOLF CLUB

These pioneers wasted no time in creating a six-hole course. The **Belfast Golf Club**, as it was known, proved to be an immediate success. The first eighteen-hole competition took place on the new course on Boxing Day 1881. In 1885, it was prestigiously granted the favour of HRH the prince of Wales, and was thereafter known as **Royal Belfast Golf Club**.

Royal Patronage
The nineteenth century saw royal patronage given to golfing societies. The first to be honoured was Perth Golfing Society in 1833. King William IV allowed the society to include 'royal' in its title. In the following year, patronage was extended to the Society of St Andrews Golfers and the name was changed to the **Royal and Ancient Golf Club of St Andrews**. Today, there are 63 'royal' golf clubs, all of which owe that title to the British royal family.

Holywood Clubhouse

In 1917, the entire Henry Harrison estate was sold to Grainger Brothers and, in 1928, Holywood Golf Club finally bought it outright. A clubhouse was built behind the Irish Hill tee hole and used until 1923. Later an extra piece of land was added and the golf course was enlarged, without actually increasing the nine-hole layout.

Landscape and Course

In 1924, the course was extended to create an 18-hole golf course. To maintain the condition of the greens, it was necessary to have two horses to pull the machinery to cover the newly extended grounds.

1924 was a very stormy year and continual rain made the fairways, especially those on the new part of the course, very soft. Members complained about the large number of deep hoof marks and it was decided by the committee that 'leather boots be purchased for both horses'.

As a result of a fire that destroyed the clubhouse in 1945, many of the records of the club's early life were lost.

A match tee-off in front of the old clubhouse, 25 June 1924
HOLYWOOD GOLF CLUB

Holywood Golf Club Livestock

From the earliest days of the golf course, it was the custom to secure extra income by letting the land for sheep grazing. Every year, advertisements were taken out in the *Belfast News-Letter* inviting tenders to be submitted. Competition was keen. Surviving records show that in 1924 a bid of £135 *per annum* was accepted from Mr Moffat, equivalent to over £4,000 today.

There were occasional hazards for animals grazing on a golf course. In a letter to the committee, Mr Moffat complained that three of his lambs had been killed. Their deaths had been caused, in his opinion, by 'golf balls in flight'. The committee doubted this, but agreed to put up a notice in the clubhouse asking players to exercise the greatest possible care in order to avoid such incidents. A reply was sent to Mr Moffat expressing regret for his loss.

Holywood Golf Club Centenary Book

Famously, Rory showed his exasperation when he told a commentator who had questioned his caddy J.P. Fitzgerald's course management to 'shut up', calling him 'a failed golfer'. Rory declared, 'He's more than a caddy, he's my friend.'

Rory and J.P. Fitzgerald check out the lie of the land on the tenth green at Killarney Golf and Fishing Club, July 2010.
INPHO/CATHAL NOONAN

Rory and J.P.

Today's caddy is at the very centre of the professional golfing game strategy. A mentor, confidant and skilful assessor of the course, J.P. Fitzgerald plays a vital role in helping to maintain motivation, confidence, attention and positive thinking so Rory can play his best game.

Rory has remained steadfastly loyal to J.P. who was widely criticised in 2011 when Rory was defeated at the **US Masters Tournament**.

Early Caddying at Holywood Golf Club

As golf was a pastime of the middle and upper classes, 'gentlemen' did not carry bags. They hired caddies. Most, if not all, clubs had a caddy master and an official list of recognised club caddies. There was a complex procedure for acquiring qualified status. The long-serving Joe McCartney was one of the most popular caddy masters at Holywood Golf Club. He was responsible for training and accountable for the caddies' behaviour. He gave aspiring young lads clear and detailed instruction on what would be required of them. The usual things were to give helpful advice on the lines of shots and putts, to stand on tees, greens and fairways, and to remain still and quiet during play.

Holywood Golf Club Centenary Book

Don'ts for Golfers

Don't despise a hint from your caddy because he is a 'wee bit of a laddie'. Most of those youngsters have acquired more first-hand knowledge of the game from caddying for good players than you will ever assimilate from a textbook. (Sandy Green, *Don'ts for Golfers*, 1926)

Caddy Turned Professional

Back in the 1930s, a likely lad with the right qualifications could earn himself a shilling by caddying on a Saturday afternoon. There was always the possibility of a couple of extra pennies by way of a performance-related tip. The early caddies lived and died on the golf course. Skill in spotting the 'line' and landing area of every shot was a crucial requirement. The caddy was expected to be standing by the ball when his player arrived, whether on the fairway, in the rough or in a hazard. A good caddy took pride in not losing a ball during a round.

In those early days at Holywood, a new recruit had to caddy for a full round for Mr McCartney. If McCartney was satisfied, the boy became a club caddy.

While waiting for the hoped-for call to accompany a player on Saturday afternoons, most caddies practised chipping and putting. Some of the best players in later years began as caddies. An ex-caddy tended to have a good short game and a lot of experience gained from observing how not to play.

Many turned professional. In 1913, one former American caddy, Francis Ouimet, shocked the golfing world when he won the **US Open Championship**. Francis Ouimet was an amateur player from a working-class family who defeated his golfing idol and childhood hero, the defending British champion Harry Vardon, at the **Country Club**, Brookline, Massachusetts in 1913.

At 20 years old, the former caddy was relatively unknown but supremely talented. He became America's first golfing hero. The self-taught Ouimet toppled the British powerhouse in a playoff victory. He changed the sport forever, and made possible the dreams of kids from any walk of life who thought they must have what it takes to win one of the most coveted titles in world sport.

Rory McIlroy and Tiger Woods eyeball each other before their one-day golf challenge in Zhengzhou, Henan Province, China in October 2012.
MARK RALSTON/AFP/GETTY IMAGES

Playing with Tiger

Playing your hero is a rare dream come true. Rory's performance when he played against his hero Tiger Woods echoes that of Ouimet over a hundred years ago. Rory defeated Woods by one stroke in the first one-to-one exhibition match between golf's two biggest names at **Jinsha Lake Golf Club** in central China on 29 October 2012.

The event, dubbed 'Duel at Jinsha Lake', marked the first time the two golfers had played head to head without other competitors. It certainly will not be their last golfing battle.

'Caddy' or **'caddie'** derives from the French word *cadet*, meaning 'young nobleman'. Because golf balls were so expensive in the past, golfers employed 'forecaddies' to stand where the ball might land (in the rough) to reduce the number of lost balls. To draw the forecaddie's attention to the fact that the ball was coming in his direction, the golfer would call out, 'Fore!'

www.flyingbluegolf.com

In the late nineteenth century, the life of a golfing professional was an arduous one.

Golf was still largely an informal game with almost no distinction between amateurs and professionals. Matches were set up primarily with bets made between players and spectators. Some of the best early professionals only made between 7 and 17 shillings per week (the equivalent of £20–£50 today).

The organisation of matches changed with the advent of a new event played on 17 October 1860: the **Open Championship**. Also called the **British Open**, this 36-hole tournament was played at **Prestwick Golf Club**, South Ayrshire, Scotland. Amateurs were not allowed to enter the first Open, and professional golfers were not common at this time, so the first field included only eight players.

Willie Park Senior, one of the pioneers of professional golf, won with a score of 174, beating the favourite, Old Tom Morris, by two strokes. The early winners were all Scottish professionals. In those days they worked as greenskeepers, clubmakers and caddies to supplement their modest winnings from championships and challenge matches. The following year the tournament was opened to amateurs; eight of them joined ten professionals in the field. Originally, the trophy presented to the event's winner was the Challenge Belt, a red leather belt with a silver buckle. In 1863, a prize fund of £10 was introduced, which was shared between the second, third and fourth-placed professionals, with the champion still only getting to keep the belt for a year. In 1864 Old Tom Morris won the first champion's cash prize of £6.

Holywood golf professional Paddy Frawley with his wife Maureen, outside the professional's shop
HOLYWOOD GOLF CLUB

The first professional to be employed at Holywood Golf Club was Bunty Haskins. He was succeeded by Joe McCartney – a great character as well as a superb golfer, who was Ulster champion on several occasions. After Joe McCartney left, Jack McCourt combined the jobs of club professional and greenskeeper, as did Paddy Frawley after him. Both were excellent club servants, keeping the course in pristine condition.

New Era

In the mid-twentieth century, a new era of professionalism emerged and the professional became a full-time post. He was now required to play in competitions and tend members' requirements by supplying clubs and clothing and offering repair services at what was called from then on the club's pro shop.

Hughie Hill, greenskeeper and professional
HOLYWOOD GOLF CLUB

I think he was just dreaming from a young age.

'When I was the professional here at Holywood and I had the shop, Rory was just a young boy. He would come into my shop two or three times a week. He would stand at the counter and lift the scorecard. At the top he would write 'British Open Championship' and then he would write his name and record scores on each of the holes. He would always have shot a great score, usually achieving seven or eight under par.

At the end of the round he would sign his name in the player's box and in the other box he would write 'Tiger Woods' or 'Nick Faldo' or the name of another famous golfer he imagined himself playing with that day.

I think he was really dreaming from a young age.'

Paul Gray, golf pro at Holywood Golf Club for 11 years, is now the manager, running the club shop and overseeing the junior programme. A product of the Michael Bannon juvenile coaching regime himself, he witnessed young Rory's ambition first hand.
HOLYWOOD GOLF CLUB

The pro shop – the natural place to be
PRIVATE FAMILY COLLECTION

'My first memory of Rory would have been seeing him up here in the lounge area of Holywood Golf Club when he was just three or four years of age. I used to run a competition called the Prima Cup for the members. His dad won it a few times. I always presented the winner with a cup. One Sunday wee Rory was here, holding the cup his father had received. Rory was delighted and brimming with pride. I remember wondering if that would be Rory himself in a few years time.'

Michael Eaton, HGC captain, March 2012–March 2013

Michael Eaton with Rory
MICHAEL EATON

That's the way we were woken up in the morning – banged over the head with a plastic golf club. Rosie McIlroy

'Par' is the number of strokes an expert golfer is expected to need to complete an individual hole, or all the holes on a golf course. On a par-three hole, an expert golfer is expected to need only one stroke to reach the green, followed by two putts. On a par-four hole, he or she should need two strokes to reach the green, followed by two putts and so on.

Brent Kelley at golfabout.com

Paul Gray, Holywood Golf Club's general manager, recalls, 'When Rory was still in a pram his father Gerry would park him at the driving range. Rory's dad was a very good golfer in his day. Gerry would take half an hour to hit some balls two to three times a week. He would look after Rory if Rosie was working and he would put the pram in front of himself. Even then, Rory was dying to get out of the buggy to try this thing that his dad was doing, though he probably didn't know what it was at the time.'

Gerry encouraging 18-month-old Rory on Holywood Golf Course
PRIVATE FAMILY COLLECTION

Interviewed in 2006, Rory's mother Rosie was convinced of his talent, 'He's been talking about this since he was two years of age. "I want to be a professional golfer," he'd say. He'd have the golf magazines out on the floor and he'd go from page to page and find a picture of Nick Faldo and point and say, "Nick Faldo". He used to call himself Rory "Nick Faldo" McIlroy. He had the little plastic clubs when he was a wee baby and we were going through a set a week because he was hitting hard balls. He didn't want to play with plastic balls; he wanted to play with hard ones! He was in the paper when he was 18 months old because Gerry had some cut-down clubs made for him. He was still in nappies, I remember. I worked during the day and Gerry worked at night. So Gerry would be away up to Holywood Golf Club during the day. They would stay on the golf course all day. Rory was holding a golf club before he could walk.'

Paul Gray recalls, 'When I was a junior member here at 18 or 19 and Rory was only a toddler, his dad and mum used to come up for dinner on Sunday nights. He could barely walk, but he used to play in here. Some of the members would get quite disgruntled as they were trying to have a quiet meal. It's something you couldn't get away with nowadays, but twenty years ago he did.'

'I started playing with Rory when he was about eight or nine years old. I recall the first time I was out with him on Holywood Golf Course. It was 1998. I was going to play at Portrush later that day, so I was practising on holes 17 and 18. Rory asked if he could join me and I said, "Sure, c'mon, Rory." So we headed off and he hit a drive down and ended up parring the hole. He said it was the first time he had ever done that. Nowadays, he can nearly drive that hole. But that was his first ever par … Amazing.'

Michael Eaton, HGC captain, March 2012–March 2013

Michael Bannon at Holywood Golf Club, 1986
HOLYWOOD GOLF CLUB

Michael Bannon began coaching Rory when Rory was about eight years of age. Although Bannon left Holywood in 1999 to join **Bangor Golf Club**, Gerry McIlroy and Bannon remained great friends. It was decided that the partnership should continue. Gerry recognised Bannon's extraordinary coaching ability. This was vital to the story of Rory's progress and his development towards becoming a champion.

Rory was undoubtedly a natural player. Bannon preserved his fundamental game, pushing him, but not trying to change his swing or natural setup. The aim was simply to nurture and hone Rory's burgeoning talent.

Rory constantly quizzed his swing coach about every aspect of the game, so he could absorb even the minutest detail. He was eager to learn about swing and grip.

Michael Eaton recalls, 'Gerry went up to bed one night after Rory had been with Bannon on the golf course having yet another lesson. Rory was fast asleep with his hands still holding the golf clubs in the grip Michael Bannon had taught him to practise. That's dedication. Bannon still knows Rory's game inside out. He knows what to say to him and Rory responds to that. It's a rare bond.'

Bannon started at Holywood Golf Club in 1983. Sam Bacon was the professional at the time, who passed on the baton to Bannon.

'I suspect he learned a lot listening to Sam Bacon,' says Michael Eaton. 'Sam Bacon was a wily old man and great amateurs like Garth McGimpsey used to visit him. Michael certainly learnt a lot from him, and has passed on that valuable knowledge to Rory.'

The thing I like about Michael is he's quiet, he's humble, he doesn't like the spotlight. He just wants me to swing my best and play my best. He's not really looking for anything out of it. Rory

Ten year-old Rory McIlroy gets in a practice round at Holywood Golf Club with club professional Michael Bannon.
PACEMAKER PRESS

Working toward a common goal bonded teacher and student. Bannon became like family. 'He knows Rory's whole personality, his golf game, inside out,' says Gerry. 'I would even say Michael knows Rory as well as I do.'

'If I told him about some problem, he'd come back in a week or two and he'd have it fixed,' says Bannon.'

Alan Bastable, Senior Editor GOLF Magazine October 2012; golf.com

Michael Bannon began playing golf at the age of seven turning professional in 1981. He went on to win more than 20 titles on the Irish Region Tour, a club pro circuit.

When Bannon started working at **Holywood Golf Club** he became friendly with Gerry and Rosie McIlroy. It was then he started coaching Rory and focusing on his swing. Bannon would record Rory's swing on a camera and they would examine it together in great detail to enhance his swing technique. In a rare interview with GOLF magazine, Bannon explains his unique relationship with Rory today and those early years:

'Even in the wintertime, Rory would come down once a month or once every two weeks. He always pushed himself. He would have said, "I think I need to go see Michael. I think I need to do this." It wasn't as if he had to come. He didn't need to do that. And even today it's the same way.'

Michael Bannon on 1 July 2012, during the final round of the 2012 Irish Open, held on the Dunluce Links at Royal Portrush Golf Club
DAVID CANNON/GETTY IMAGES

You can get coached all you want, but you have to make your golf swing your own, and Michael has let me do that. Rory

In 2011, Michael Bannon was named the European PGA Golf Coach of the Year and now coaches Rory full time.

Ten-year-old Rory with Michael Bannon

PACEMAKER PRESS

25

Rory's burning ambition and reputation for hard work and persistence are born of a family work ethic built on sheer grind and graft.

Rory's grandfather, Jimmy McIlroy, worked endless shifts and long hours on the historic Harland & Wolff shipyard on Belfast's Queen's Island, famous for the construction of the RMS *Titanic*. Jimmy repaired the gantry cranes known as Samson and Goliath.

Jimmy's son Gerry grew up just a thousand yards from Holywood Golf Club. He developed a great appetite for the game, playing with his father and two brothers. As a near-scratch golfer, Gerry played at least two or three times every week. He was club champion and one of the top players.

'I've known the whole family for about 35 years – especially Jimmy. He just loved the game. He worked in the shipyards and most nights came up to play with his sons Gerry and Colm. I remember joining Jimmy in the early to mid-1980s with them. Jimmy passed away three weeks after he retired in 1991. It was a pity, as Rory was just a wee baby. He would have loved to see how well his grandson has done. If his grandfather hadn't been a member here, then Gerry wouldn't have been a member – and perhaps we might not have had Rory McIlroy the golfer.'

Michael Eaton, HGC captain,
March 2012–March 2013

A **'handicap'** is a numerical representation of an amateur golfer's playing ability. The lower the handicap, the better the golfer is. It is based on the number of strokes by which he or she usually exceeds par for a course, although it is meant to represent potential rather than simply be an average of a golfer's scores. Handicap indexes are used so that golfers of different playing abilities can compete fairly against one another.

www.about.com

The 'James Brothers', winners of the Belfast and District Golf Snooker League 1973–4. Rory's grandfather Jimmy McIlroy (centre) with Jimmy Hewitt, Jimmy Coleman, Jimmy Curtis, Jimmy Ralph, Jimmy Donnelly and Jimmy White.
HOLYWOOD GOLF CLUB

'Scratch golfer', in common usage, means the golfer being referred to has a handicap of zero or below. Another way of putting it: a 'scratch golfer' is one whose average score for a round of golf is par or better. When used by golfers discussing handicaps, 'scratch golfer' is sometimes shortened to just 'scratch'.

Gerry with the Holywood Senior Cup Team, 1981, at Knock Golf Club: (Left–right) Willie Craven, Gerry McIlroy, Eamon Carty, Wilber Walker and Patrick Mitchel
HOLYWOOD GOLF CLUB

Rory's uncle, Colm McIlroy, with Rory's grandfather Jimmy, featured in the local paper for having shot a hole in one at ten years old.
PRIVATE FAMILY COLLECTION

Gerry McIlroy married Rosie at St Colmcille's Church, Holywood on 13 January 1988. The following year, on 4 May 1989, Rory was born. He was later baptised at the church where they were wed. To help make ends meet, Rosie returned to work on the nightshift at the 3M factory in Bangor. Gerry cleaned the locker rooms at a rugby and cricket club in the mornings, worked as a bartender in the afternoon, and returned to work at the rugby club bar until midnight.

CLUB CHAMPIONS
Club Championship Trophy. Presented by Hugh C. Meharg 1953

1953	W.S. STEVENSON	1981	S. THOMPSON	2009	T. DUN
1954	C. GRAHAM	1982	J. DICKSON	2010	T. DUN
1955	J.FD. MADELEY	1983	P. MITCHEL	2011	J. GOU
1956	J.FD. MADELEY	1984	S. KING	2012	J. GOU
1957	J.B. BALLAGH	1985	D. McCARTNEY	2013	
1958	P.A. BOYLE	1986	E. CARTY	2014	
1959	P.W. LENNOX	1987	P. GREENE	2015	
1960	D.J. KITSON	1988	S. KING	2016	
1961	T.J. BALMER	1989	S. KING	2017	
1962	B. DUFFIN	1990	C. McILROY	2018	
1963	J. WATTS	1991	P. COLLINS	2019	
1964	J. WATTS	1992	T. DUNLOP	2020	
1965	W. GILPIN	1993	G. McILROY	2021	
1966	J. WATTS	1994	J. DICKSON	2022	
1967	J. WATTS	1995	J. DICKSON	2023	
1968	J. WATTS	1996	T. McCLEMENTS	2024	
1969	J. WATTS	1997	I. SMYTH	2025	
1970	J. DICKSON	1998	M. EATON	2026	
1971	P.J. KELLY	1999	A. WATT	2027	
1972	J. WATTS	2000	T. McCLEMENTS	2028	
1973	J. WATTS	2001	J. DICKSON	2029	
1974	H. MAGEE	2002	T. McCLEMENTS	2030	
1975	J. DICKSON	2003	G. DICKSON	2031	
1976	J. DICKSON	2004	I. SMYTH	2032	
1977	T. McNEIL	2005	R. McILROY	2033	
1978	A.P. McMASTER	2006	T. McCLEMENTS	2034	
1979	W. CRAVEN	2007	T. McCLEMENTS	2035	
1980	S. KING	2008	C. McILROY	2036	

ABOVE: The Board of Honour in the bar at Holywood Golf Club, featuring the McIlroy family through the years
DERMOTT DUNBAR

Rosie, Rory and Gerry at Rosses Point, County Sligo, when Rory won the West of Ireland Championship, 2005
PRIVATE FAMILY COLLECTION

A **'hole in one'** is a rare feat, which the average amateur golfer will probably never achieve. *Golf Digest* and the National Hole in One Association estimate that a tee shot hit by an amateur golfer on a par-3 hole goes into the hole once every 12,750 times. With such astronomical odds, it is even more amazing to read tales of players with two holes in one in a round or short period of time. On a course that features four par-three holes, a player would make two holes in one in a round once every 162,562,500 times, according to *Golf Digest*.

He was a child prodigy.

The endless practice and coaching with Michael Bannon began to pay dividends. Rory's talent was astonishing.

Gerry also taught Rory a lot. Very much like Tiger Woods's father, he would try to distract him to make him learn to focus totally on his game. He took him through his paces and would say, 'Right Rory, hit this fade, hit this draw, hit it straight' – and Rory would try.

Earl Woods (Tiger's father) met the young Rory in 1999 at the Junior World Golf Championships in Miami, Florida.
PRIVATE FAMILY COLLECTION

Tiger Woods as a two-year-old golf prodigy on *The Mike Douglas Show*, 6 October 1978
CBS VIA GETTY IMAGES

Tiger Woods

The parallels between the early golfing life of Rory and his idol Tiger Woods are remarkable. Both were golfing prodigies mentored by their fathers. Like Rory, Woods was an only child. His father Earl was an army officer. Named Eldrick Tont, when Woods was a child, his father began calling him 'Tiger' in honour of a fellow soldier and friend.

By the age of eight, Woods was extremely proficient at golf. Like Rory, as a young boy Woods demonstrated his skills on television shows, such as *Good Morning America*. Woods won a number of amateur US golf titles before turning professional in 1996. He shot to fame at the age of 21 after winning the **US Masters Tournament** at Augusta in 1997 with a record score of 270. Woods was the youngest man to earn the title.

Rory was delighted to meet Tiger's father at the **Junior World Golf Championships** in 1999.

The nine-year-old Rory's swing
ALAN LEWIS

Once Gerry saw Rory's determination, he just threw in everything he had to support him. Paul Gray, general manager, Holywood Golf Club

Rory in 2005 in Holywood with Gerry and Rosie

PACEMAKER PRESS

Rory would putt long into the night on a practice green his parents planted over the garden and the front yard of their red-brick home. After watching an instructional tape, he started calling himself Rory 'Nick Faldo' McIlroy.

Rory's teacher at St Patrick's Primary School, Maighread McCullough, recalled how golf-mad he was: 'I remember in the summer time he was usually on the golf course before he came to school and then he went golfing after school. He always had golf balls and tees in his pockets.'

The McIlroys' garden in Holywood

ALAN LEWIS

Rory – a world champion at just nine years old. He won the World Under-Ten Championship with a record score, finishing level par after three rounds of one under, one over and level par, to win by five strokes.

On his ninth birthday, Rory met one of his golfing heroes, Darren Clarke OBE, at the **Royal Portrush Golf Club**. This was to be the start of a lifelong friendship that began through the **Darren Clarke Foundation**.

'He stood out straight away,' says Clarke. 'He didn't hit quite as far as he hits now. As a professional, you can always spot someone who has got the talent, but you don't know who is going to make it and who is not going to make it. I pretty much knew what he was doing from a very young age.'

RORY
KEEP UP THE
GOOD WORK.

BEST WISHES
Darren Clarke

PRIVATE FAMILY COLLECTION

The Darren Clarke Foundation was set up in 2002 to introduce the game of golf to children of all ages in all parts of Ireland. Apart from lending his expert skill and knowledge of the game to youngsters like Rory, the foundation is also committed to raising money for various cancer charities. The charity is close to Darren Clarke's heart. He lost his first wife Heather in August 2006 after she was diagnosed with cancer in 2002.

'I remember when Darren first saw Rory hitting a single great shot as a young kid. I think Darren thought it was a one-off. But Rory kept repeating that particular swing. Darren realised that Rory's talent was incredibly natural. In golf a lot of the technique is about club-head speed, delivery of the club to the ball and positioning. Rory had a great knowledge and understanding of these elements, very much like all the great players of the game.'

Michael Eaton, HGC captain, March 2012–March 2013

Rory tees off as Darren Clarke looks on during the final practice round of the Open Championship at Royal St George's, Sandwich, England, on 13 July 2011. Clarke went on to a spectacular win at that 140th Open tournament.

STUART FRANKLIN/GETTY IMAGES

Remember the swing and remember the name, for, at just nine years old, Rory McIlroy from Holywood is following in the steps of his golfing hero, Tiger Woods.

These were prophetic words from BBC news reporter Rod Nawn when he interviewed Rory in 1998. Michael Bannon told Rod, 'He has a great head on his shoulders. He has a great future ahead of him, I think, not only in golf but in life as well. There is not a day goes by that Rory doesn't hit a ball, swing a club, grip a club or think about it.'

World Masters of Junior Golf,
Hawaii, 1999
PRIVATE FAMILY COLLECTION

Not only was Rory hitting the headlines on television, but he was also winning championships. In 1999 he won the **Junior World Golf Championships** in the under-10 division with a victory at **Doral Golf Resort and Spa,** Miami, Florida.

That same year, Northern Irish television channel UTV interviewed the nine-year-old, who showed off his skills, juggling a golf ball and then chipping it into a washing machine, much to the delight of the studio audience.

Host Gerry Kelly famously closed the item by saying, 'Look out for this guy. If the Americans have Tiger Woods, we have young Rory – and what a star!'

Golf Wisdom

'You build a golf game like you build a wall. A brick at a time.'

Tony Lema

31

Ricky McCormick,
2004

I remember when he was a juvenile here. He would have been 11 and playing as a reserve. We were playing against Dunmurry. Some of the kids placed to go out against him were 15 or 16 years of age and didn't want to go. They were scared he would beat them.

Ricky McCormick, schoolfriend

Sullivan Upper Golf Club. (Front row, left–right) Stuart Cave, Rory McIlroy, Stephen Gordon; (back row, left–right) Lee Evans, Mr Dermott, Jonathan Warnock

The Ulster Schools Cup, 2002

Rory regularly represented his school club and former pupil Jonathan Warnock recalls a particularly nail-biting tournament for one of the smallest players in the field.

It was the 210-yard par-three first at **City of Derry Golf Club**, a sudden death playoff hole as Sullivan and RBAI were tied following the morning matches at 2½ each. Sullivan's number one was a 12-year old Rory McIlroy (height five feet, weight seven stone, golf handicap three).

His tee shot was deep in rough among trees on the right, 30 yards from the green. He had a bunker to cross with the narrowest of gaps in the trees to hit through. His opponent was sitting pretty on the other side of the green. It looked certain that Rory would have to get up and down or defeat was inevitable. But then, this was McIlroy, and even at that stage we knew our guy was always going to be special.

Out comes the wedge, Rory flops the ball perfectly through the trees and over the bunker and lands it on a sixpence. The ball rolls in to three feet from the pin. It's hard to do justice to such a spectacular shot. Rory's opponent, a talented player in his own right, chokes and fluffs a chip. Rory taps it for three.

We were in the afternoon final. Following the glory of beating the favourites, local rivals Bangor Grammar were never going to be a match for us and were duly steamrollered 5–0. The Ulster Schools Cup belonged to Sullivan Upper School, thanks to Rory.

Rory, aged 11, in Hawaii at the 2000 World Masters of Junior Golf. He finished in third place.
PRIVATE FAMILY COLLECTION

Reputation

Gripped by his passion, by age 11 Rory had shot level par at Holywood Golf Club. He played regularly with the club's team and was fast earning a reputation as a dangerous competitor.

Paul Gray took Rory on at Holywood when the wunderkind was 15. Did he beat the upstart? 'Of course I didn't,' he says.

In just a few short years a teenage Rory was making huge progress with record-breaking victories both at home and abroad.

Junior Tournament Memories

At **Oughterard Golf Club**, County Galway, in August 2003, Rory broke the course record at the **Connacht Boys Amateur Open Championship**.

In August 2004, he won the **Nissan Irish Boys Amateur Close Championship** at the **Castlebar Golf Club** in County Mayo.

Rory in action during the Boys Home Internationals on 7 August 2003 at Royal St David's Golf Club, Harlech, Wales
ANDREW REDINGTON/GETTY IMAGES

PRIVATE PHOTO FROM RICHARD ROBINSON

Rory with the trophy in the final of the Ulster Boys Championship, Donaghadee Golf Club – July 2003

It was then that Rory met his second important mentor – Sir Nick Faldo.

At 15 years old, Rory was a member of the **Junior Ryder Cup** winning team, representing Europe in Ohio at the **Westfield Group Country Club** on 11–12 September 2004. The team consisted of six boys and six girls.

The **Junior Ryder Cup** has been the platform from which successful professional careers have been launched for several players. The victorious 2004 Europe team convincingly beat the USA – the final score was Europe 8½ and USA 3½.

Junior Ryder Cup

The idea for the **Junior Ryder Cup** came about in 1995, when a team of Europeans played an informal exhibition match against Central New York PGA section and area juniors. Two years later, in 1997, the **Junior Ryder Cup** was formally introduced as an event in its own right, being played at **Alcaidesa Links Golf Resort** in Cádiz, Spain and won by the USA 9–7. In 1999, the contest was held at the **Country Club of New Seabury** in Cape Cod, Massachusetts, where Europe claimed victory. Europe maintained their dominance over the next five years, winning 9½–2½ at the **K Club** in County Kildare, Ireland, in 2002.

Under-15 boys' winner Rory McIlroy proudly shares the stage with his golfing hero Nick Faldo after the 2004 Faldo Series final, held on 11 October 2004 at Burhill Golf Club, Hersham, Surrey.
PRESS ASSOCIATION

33

The sound of his ball striking is amazing. It's the 'whack' that he makes. It is crisp, it is clean and it is perfect. It is the same on every single shot he makes. If there were 20 players striking a ball, and you were blindfolded, you would unquestionably know the sound of Rory's strike. Eddie McCormack, who was 32 years of age when he played against Rory in the **Irish Amateur Close Championship**. (Justin Doyle, *Rory: His Story So Far*, 2011)

Eddie McCormack, Galway Golf Club.
EDDIE McCORMACK

Rory pictured on 4 August 2004, during the Boys Home Internationals tournament in Portmarnock, Ireland
ROSS KINNAIRD/GETTY IMAGES

'Because Rory came up here to HGC and practised his short game so much, I'm surprised at how great his long game actually is. But the fact is he was so good that he had the chance to play all over Ireland, England, Scotland, Wales and around the world before he was 16 or 17. So he practised and that long game came naturally. In the beginning he wasn't known for his putting as he seemed a bit aggressive. But that has changed so much. I'm surprised that his long game is so good, as our club is not a long-game course. Rory would have had to go to the driving range and practise his long game with great dedication.

'He is one in ten million. His flexibility and strength are a rare combination. Ben Hogan and Seve Ballesteros had that great par game. I think Rory's speed coming into the ball is around 120 miles per hour. The average speed is 80 to 100 miles per hour. It's all about his power coming into the turn, the pivot of his hips and his timing in terms of contact with the ball. I'm not sure you can teach that. Even when he was 15 or 16 he could hit the ball a mile. It's just frightening how well he could do that.'

Michael Eaton, HGC captain, March 2012–March 2013

In 2005, Rory became the youngest ever winner of the **West of Ireland Amateur Open Championship** at **County Sligo Golf Club**, Rosses Point, and of the **Irish Amateur Close Championship,** held at **Westport Golf Club** in County Mayo.

Rory tees off on the fifth in the Interprovincial Championship at County Sligo Golf Club, Rosses Point, on 11 August 2005.
COUNTY SLIGO GOLF CLUB

Rory about to take the winning putt for the Irish Amateur Close Championship at Westport, 2005
WESTPORT GOLF CLUB

Part of the winning team of the Belfast and District Cup, 2004, at Spa Golf Club, Ballynahinch, County Down
CONNOR ASTON

Like his heroes Tiger Woods and Nick Faldo, Rory decided it was golf or nothing – even if he didn't always have a winning hand.

The year 2005 proved to be crucial time for Rory. He made a life-changing decision just two months shy of his sixteenth birthday.

'Rory was in the year above me. At school he was just like the others until he got to fifth year, when he was away a lot. It was then that he decided to leave school before his GCSE exams.'

Rory and his close friend Ricky travelling together in the US, spring 2013
RICKY McCORMICK

'I actually caddied quite a lot for him. I remember we played on the golf team together. We had a very good golf team. It was Rory and two guys who were off scratch and myself, off two. Actually, Rory got beaten in the first match by a five-handicapper and he was off +5. He had to tell his dad that I lost because he said his dad wouldn't be too happy. I don't think Gerry knows that to this day. From the four matches it was 2–2. I was in the car on the way home when he said, "Yeah, I won and Ricky lost." He just didn't want to disappoint his father.'

Ricky McCormick, PGA professional, HGC, 2013

Language of Golf
'Golf is a game where the ball always lies poorly and the player always lies well.'
ANONYMOUS

By all accounts, Rory didn't disappoint Gerry. On 12 May 2005, a few days after turning 16, he made his first appearance in a European Tour event when he took part in the **British Masters**. It was his first pro tournament.

John Stevenson was principal at Rory's high school, Sullivan Upper, Holywood. As well as witnessing the teenage golf prodigy, he saw what he terms 'the first post-Troubles generation' come to maturity.

'They seem much more interested in their economic future than anything else,' he said. 'You could press them as to whether they want to live in an all-Ireland state, and they would have different views. But it doesn't seem to be locked into their identity, as it maybe was for a previous generation. There is an energy about the place, and Rory is leading that to a certain extent.' 10 July 2011 *New York Times*

LEFT: Sixteen year-old Rory teeing off at the Nissan Irish Open at Carton House Golf Club, Maynooth, County Kildare, on 19–22 May 2005. The prize money was over €2 million.
PACEMAKER PRESS

In July 2005, Rory took part in the **North of Ireland Amateur Open Championship** on the **Dunluce Links** at **Royal Portrush Golf Club** and played such sensational golf that he hit the headlines. He shot a new competitive course record score of 61, a whopping 11 under par, with nine birdies and an eagle, bettering the previous best around the links by an incredible three shots.

'I can basically remember every shot. I remember I missed a six-footer on the first for a birdie and that could have been better. Just one of those days where everything is on song. I turned on 3-under, birdied 9, eagled 10, birdied 11, parred 12 and 13, and then birdied my way in. Basically I didn't miss a shot from there.' Rory McIlroy

Rory beaming after his round of 61 at Royal Portrush in 2005.
HARRY MARCUS

'Birdie' is the term for a score of one under par on any individual golf hole. According to Peter Davies's *The Historical Dictionary of Golfing Terms* (1992), 'Birdie comes from the 19th century American slang term "bird" meaning anything excellent.'

'Eagle' means a score of two under par for a given hole. It was clearly an extension of the theme of birds for good scores derived from 'birdie'. A score of two under par can be seen as a large birdie and an eagle, after all, is a big bird.

Scottish Golf History

In 2005, Rory also became the youngest ever winner of both the **West of Ireland Amateur Open Championship** and the **Irish Amateur Close Championship**.

Rory's golfing achievements at the end of 2005 were acknowledged when he was presented with the *Irish Examiner* Junior Golfer of the Year award.

Throughout 2006 Rory continued to improve his game and gather experience. He had his eyes firmly fixed on playing alongside his professional heroes.

He defended his title as champion of the **West of Ireland Amateur Open Championship** and of the **Irish Amateur Close Championship**. In August, he became European amateur champion at **Golf Club Biella** near Milan. In October, he represented Ireland in the **Eisenhower Trophy**, the amateur world team championship, in South Africa.

2007 turned out to be a very special year for Rory.

Early in 2007, Rory made his first cut in a professional tournament as an amateur. It happened at the European Tour's **Dubai Desert Classic** at the **Emirates Golf Club**, Dubai, United Arab Emirates in February. He opened with back-to-back scores of 69, then shot 71 and 76. He finished tied for fifty-second place. He was just 17 years and 10 months old.

Rory hits his second shot on the seventeenth hole during the second round of the Dubai Desert Classic on 2 February 2007, on the Majlis Course at Emirates Golf Club, Dubai
ANDREW REDINGTON/GETTY IMAGE

Rory continued to hone his game on the amateur circuit for the best part of 2007.

In June, he took part in the **Amateur Championship**, one of the two leading individual tournaments for amateur golfers, (alongside the **US Amateur Championship**) at **Royal Lytham and St Annes Golf Club**, Lancashire, England. In early July, he played in the **European Amateur Team Championship**, held at **Western Gailes Golf Club**, Ayrshire, Scotland.

Rory selects a club on the fourth hole during the Amateur Championship on 19 June 2007 at Royal Lytham and St Annes Golf Club, England.
ANDREW REDINGTON/GETTY IMAGES

Rory drives at the tenth hole during the second round of the strokeplay qualifying for the 2007 European Amateur Team Championship, held at Western Gailes Golf Club, Scotland on 4 July 2007.
DAVID CANNON/GETTY IMAGES

Later in July, at the **Carnoustie Golf Links**, Angus, Scotland, Rory entered the record books as the first amateur from Ireland to make the **Open Championship** cut since Joe Carr in 1965. His performance put him firmly in the public eye.

41

Many professional golfers have criticised Carnoustie for its severity, nicknaming it 'Carnasty' because of its difficulty, especially under adverse weather conditions. It is considered by many to be one of the toughest courses in the world.

Rory watches a shot from the rough on the second hole during the second round of the 136th Open Championship at Carnoustie Golf Links, Scotland, on 20 July 2007.

Golf was never meant to be a fair game, or an easy one. We've got the reputation as being a beastly test, but that's what golf is – it's a beastly test.
Carnoustie's head greenskeeper, John Philip

The Carnoustie Effect

The term 'Carnoustie effect' dates from the 1999 **Open Championship**, when the world's best players struggled with the notoriously difficult course and weather conditions. Inspired by this event, in his book *The Carnoustie Effect: Warfare in the 21st Century*, published in 2002, Scottish author Gordon Lang coined the term to describe the 'psychic shock experienced on collision with reality by those whose expectations are founded on false assumptions.' This can, of course, apply to disillusionment in any area of activity, not just in golf.

Rory was one of only six amateurs in the field. Incredibly, the prodigy began beating his own golfing mentors. As the competition progressed, he was eleven strokes ahead of Nick Faldo and four strokes ahead of Darren Clarke. He was also closing in on his biggest hero – Tiger Woods. Just eight months earlier, Rory had been tentatively standing on the sidelines, watching his hero with awe. Now, at just one stroke behind him, Rory was standing toe to toe with his all-time golfing idol. Ultimately, Rory tied for forty-second position, shooting 3 under par 68 as an opening tee and triumphing with a silver medal for the leading amateur.

Tiger Woods follows through on a tee shot during the second round of the 136th Open Championship in Carnoustie, 20 July 2007.
DARREN CARROLL/GETTY IMAGES   43

Early September 2007 saw Rory's last days as an amateur.

Local boys Jonathan Caldwell and Rory pose at the nose of their plane, as the Great Britain and Ireland Walker Cup team lands at George Best Belfast City Airport to prepare for their match against the United States at the Royal County Down Golf Club, Newcastle.
CHARLES McQUILLAN/PACEMAKER

Walker Cup

The **Walker Cup** is contested biennially in odd-numbered years between leading amateur golfers of the United States, Great Britain and Ireland. The event is named in honour of George Herbert Walker, grandfather of George H.W. Bush, forty-first president of the United States, and great-grandfather of George W. Bush, forty-third president of the United States. George Herbert Walker was president of the United States Golf Association in 1920, when the series was initiated.

Getting closer to Tiger Woods at Carnoustie was a dream come true for Rory. It turned out to be one of many, as he set his sights on joining his golfing heroes on the professional circuit.

On 8 September 2007, Rory played with the Great Britain and Ireland team in the forty-first **Walker Cup** contest. Hosted at the **Royal County Down Golf Club**, Newcastle, Northern Ireland, this proved to be his last amateur tournament.

Rory was in buoyant spirits and enjoyed the camaraderie with his teammates.

Rory and playing partner Jonathan Caldwell during their practice round ahead of the Walker Cup at the Royal County Down Golf Club.
CHARLES McQUILLAN/PACEMAKER

Rory played with Jonathan Caldwell and halved with Colt Knost/Dustin Johnson of the US, who went on to beat Great Britain and Ireland 13½ to 12½.
CHARLES McQUILLAN/PACEMAKER

Despite the tournament defeat, in 2007 Rory was number one in the world amateur rankings. After a hectic year, Rory was very clear about his golfing ambitions.

On 19 September 2007, Rory turned professional.

He was just 18 years old.

Rory watches, dejected, with Jonathan Caldwell after a defeat during his foursomes match against the United States at the Royal County Down Golf Club, Newcastle.
CHARLES McQUILLAN/PACEMAKER

I'm not playing for money.
I'm playing for a place in history.

Rory

Only four days later, on 22 September, Rory teed off in his first tournament, the **Quinn Direct British Masters**, on the European Tour at **the Belfry** in Warwickshire. Despite a second-round score of 78, Rory made the cut. He shot rounds of 69, 78, 70 and 73 to finish at 2 over par 290, and tied for forty-second place.

In his second professional event, in October 2007, Rory finished in third position at the **Alfred Dunhill Links Championship** at the **Old Course, St Andrews, Carnoustie** and **Kingsbarns**.

Rory's brilliant start to his professional career continued with a share of fourth place in the **Open de Madrid Valle Romano**. At the **Real Sociedad Hípica Española Club de Campo** near Madrid, on 11 October, Rory carded a final round 70 to finish five shots behind Denmark's Mads Vibe-Hastrup. Rory was bidding to become the youngest winner in European Tour history at 18 years and 163 days old. He had a rollercoaster round of five birdies, one eagle and five bogeys. It was another impressive performance in just his third event in the paid ranks.

'I think I have done well after all that has gone over the last few weeks. There was a lot to contend with so finishing in the top five is pretty good. I'm hitting it really well. If I could get a couple more putts to drop it would make the difference. That's me probably into the top 100 on the Order of Merit now, so I am happy. Onwards and upwards.'

Order of Merit

The European Tour's money list was known as the Order of Merit until 2009, when it was replaced by the Race to Dubai. It is calculated in euro, although around half of the events have prize funds that are fixed in other currencies, mainly pounds sterling or US dollars. In these instances, the amounts are converted into euro at the exchange rate for the week when the tournament is being played. The winner of the Order of Merit receives the Harry Vardon Trophy (not to be confused with the Vardon Trophy, awarded by the PGA of America).

Rory in action on the eighteenth green during the first round of the Open de Madrid Valle Romano at the Real Sociedad Hípica Española Club de Campo on 11 October 2007
IAN WALTON/GETTY IMAGES

Rory embarked on his first full European Tour season in November 2007 when he played in the UBS Hong Kong Open. He missed the cut by just four shots.

In his first 11 events of the tour, Rory went on to miss five more cuts but held a tie for eleventh place in the **Abu Dhabi Golf Championship** on 17–20 January 2008.

As a rookie professional, Rory was making steady progress. He entered the top 200 of the Official World Golf Ranking on 27 January 2008 in 190th place. Importantly, this was an opportunity for Rory to adjust to the rigours of life on the professional circuit.

The pace picked up. In a few short months, Rory played at the **Maybank Malaysian Open**, Kuala Lumpur on 6 March; the **PGA Tour World Golf Championships** at **Doral Golf Resort and Spa**, Florida, USA on 13 March; and the **Ballantine's Championship** at **Pinx Golf Club**, Jeju Island, South Korea.

He was soon in action again at the **Open de Andalucía** near Marbella, Spain. Then it was on to the **Estoril Open de Portugal**, Cascais, on 3 April. He flew on to Shanghai for the **BMW Asian Open** at the **Tomson Shanghai Pudong Golf Club** on 24 April and then back to Ireland for the **Irish Open** at **Adare Manor Hotel and Golf Resort**, County Limerick, on 15 May.

By the time he reached the **Omega European Masters** at **Golf Club Crans-sur-Sierre**, Crans-Montana, Switzerland on 7 September 2008, Rory's play had shifted up another gear. He revealed sparks of brilliance, taking a four-stroke lead in the final round. Rory had finally acquired the look of a young contender.

He finished the tournament tying for the lead with Frenchman Jean-François Lucquin. For the first time, Rory was in a sudden-death playoff. But Rory missed his second two-putt par. Lucquin was the victor on his second hole.

En route to the Commercial Bank Qatar Masters in Dubai, Rory enjoys the Wild Wadi Water Park, 21 January 2008.

Rory plays a chip shot on the seventh hole during the second round of the Omega European Masters at Golf Club Crans-sur-Sierre, Switzerland, on 5 September 2008.

As his maiden season unfolded, Rory found himself adjusting to the disciplines of the professional golfing schedule.

'Playing the tour full time has been very different,' he admitted. 'I'm still feeling my way, but that's part of learning. The best players know how to schedule themselves at events. They play 18 holes, then go to practice knowing what they have to work on. Once they have done that they leave. What they don't do is hang around on the range taking three hours to hit 100 balls. That's just procrastination and a waste of time. The best players always have a purpose; then they get away from the game.'

John Huggan interview, *Golf Digest*, July 2008

Sentosa Golf Club, Singapore

Rory during the first round of the Barclays Singapore Open at Sentosa Golf Club on 13 November 2008

IAN WALTON/GETTY IMAGES

Rory's focus stood him in good stead. In 2008, he closed his first full European Tour season with a total of six top-ten placements. He finished second in the **UBS Hong Kong Open** in November at the **Hong Kong Golf Club**. He would return triumphant just three years later in November 2011.

In 2008, Rory ended the year thirty-ninth in the world rankings after finishing joint third in the **South African Open Championship** held at **Durban Country Club**.

EFT: Rory plays his tee shot on the third hole uring the final round of the UBS Hong Kong Open at the Hong Kong Golf Club on 23 November 2008.

TUART FRANKLIN/GETTY IMAGES

Only 18 months after turning pro, his performances earned him an invitation to the Masters Tournament in April 2009.

51

But before he could look ahead to the US Masters, Rory had to prove his mettle and go all out for a professional win. Sure enough, that first victory arrived when he won the **Omega Dubai Desert Classic** at the **Emirates Golf Club** on 1 February 2009, defeating Justin Rose by just one shot in a nail-biting playoff.

Rory poses with the trophy alongside his parents Rosie and Gerry after winning on the Majlis Course at the Emirates Golf Club.
DAVID CANNON/GETTY IMAGES

Rory dedicated the win to his parents.

'They have never been pushy. They have done so much for me and it's nice to be able to repay them in some way.'

Rory

At 19 years and 273 days old, Rory became the youngest winner of the **Omega Dubai Desert Classic**, beating the previous best of England's David Howell, who had won the 1999 edition when he was 23 years and 236 days old.

Omega Dubai Desert Classic

This competition began in 1989 when the European Tour visited Asia for the first time. The roll of honour includes seven different major champions. They are: Seve Ballesteros (1992), Ernie Els (1994, 2002, 2005), Fred Couples (1995), José Maria Olazábal (1998), Mark O'Meara (2004), Tiger Woods (2006, 2008) and Rory McIlroy (2009). Between them they have won 30 major championships.

Rory poses near his home on Holywood seafront after a press conference at his home club, Holywood, on 4 February 2009 following his maiden professional win in Dubai.
CHARLES McQUILLAN/PACEMAKER PRESS

Not one to rest on his laurels, Rory turned his sights to competing in his first ever Masters Tournament, at the Augusta National Golf Club, Georgia, in April 2009.

Holywood Golf Club Trophy Room

Among the Rory memorabilia displayed in the trophy room at Holywood Golf Club is a yellow flag hung to commemorate the thirteenth hole at **Augusta National Golf Club**. It is notorious for being one of the most difficult holes in the world of golf.

Yet Rory singled it out as one of his favourites and one that he felt he could confidently overcome.

Rory went on to eagle that infamous thirteenth hole after his second shot finished six feet from the pin. That feat is captured in a frame at Holywood Golf Club.

In 2009, Rory made 24 out of 25 cuts on the European Tour. He achieved his first win, three seconds, three thirds and a staggering fourteen top tens. By November, Rory was ninth in the Official Golf World Ranking. Now he was making headlines as a major contender with his improving form.

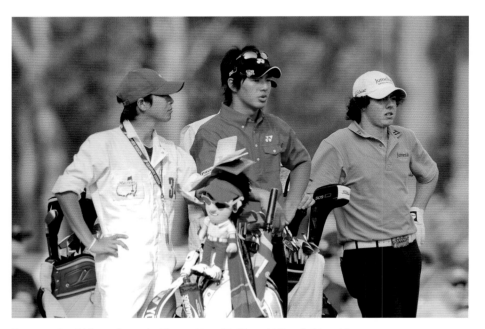

Teenagers Ryo Ishikawa (centre) of Japan, his caddy Hiroyuki Kato (left) and Rory look on apprehensively during the first round of the US Masters at the Augusta National Golf Club on 9 April 2009.

Rory played in two more events on the PGA Tour after the Masters Tournament, including his first appearance at the Players Championship (7–10 May 2009), where he missed the cut by +7.

He had famously skipped the **Players Championship** a year earlier and admitted the **TPC Sawgrass Players Stadium Course**, Ponte Vedra Beach, Florida, is one he has struggled to figure out. Not one to give up, however, Rory said he would be back to try again (in 2013). 'I promise,' he said to laughter after a 76 knocked him out of the tournament.

Rory is not alone. Many players find the home of the tour's signature event frustrating. For 19 consecutive years it has had a different winner. Since winning, Tiger Woods (2001) and Phil Mickelson (2007) have not significantly contended in the tournament.

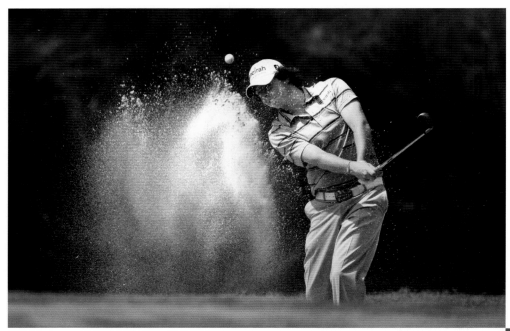

Rory plays a shot from a bunker on the seventh hole during the first round of the Players Championship on the Players Stadium Course at TPC Sawgrass, Ponte Vedra Beach, Florida, on 7 May 2009.
RICHARD HEATHCOTE/GETTY IMAGES

Rory returned to Europe and recorded two top-25 finishes leading up to his first **US Open Championship**. The first was the **BMW PGA Championship** at **Wentworth Club**, Virginia Water, Surrey, England (21–24 May 2009). Despite reacting to a poor shot during the first round, Rory went on to finish fifth in the tournament.

The following week, Rory finished twelfth in the **European Open**, held on 28–31 May at the **Heritage Golf and Spa Resort**, Killenard, County Laois, Ireland.

Rory shows his frustration during the first round of the BMW PGA Championship at Wentworth Club, Surrey on 21 May 2009.
WARREN LITTLE/GETTY IMAGES

Rory hits a shot during the first day of previews to the 109th US Open on the Black Course at Bethpage State Park, New York on 15 June 2009.
ANDREW REDINGTON/GETTY IMAGES

Luke Donald of England, Rory, Henrik Stenson of Sweden, Bernhard Langer of Germany, Martin Kaymer of Germany and Colin Montgomerie of Scotland during a press conference prior to the BMW International Open in Munich, Germany on 23 June 2009
STUART FRANKLIN/GETTY IMAGES

Second Major

By June, it was time for Rory to take on the 109th **US Open Championship**. It was to be his second major as a professional. Held on 18–22 June 2009 at **Bethpage State Park**, Farmingdale, Long Island, New York, it was the second Open to be played at Bethpage; the first had been won by Tiger Woods in 2002. The event was hit heavily by continuous rain. Rory didn't win, but his final round of 68 (–2) helped him finish in a tie for tenth place – his first top-ten finish in a major.

The following week, Rory travelled to Germany to play the **BMW International Open** held at the **Golfclub München Eichenried** in Munich (25–28 June 2009), where he finished in fifteenth place.

Hard on the heels of the **BMW International Open** came Rory's third major tournament.

Open Championship, 16–19 July 2009
Ailsa Course, Turnberry Resort, Ayrshire, Scotland

It was the fourth time the **Open Championship** had been played at **The Ailsa Course, Turnberry**, but it was Rory's first British Open as a professional. He got off to a cracking pace with a first-round score of 63. No one had ever shot a lower score and expectations were high. Rory, after all, had grown up on links golf. His previous experience of the Open had come two years earlier, when he had produced one of the great displays in the championship's recent history by recording the only bogey-free round in horrendous weather on the opening day at **Carnoustie Golf Links**.

The weather allowed Rory to score birdies at the second and seventh. But at the eighth his drive was in the rough and he struggled to make a six. Ultimately Stewart Cink won the tournament and Rory finished forty-seventh.

Rory during the practice round of the 138th Open Championship on 13 July 2009 on the Ailsa Course, Turnberry Resort, Scotland
ROSS KINNAIRD/GETTY IMAGES

'Bogey' means a score of one over par on a hole – for example, a score of five on a par-four hole. The term 'bogey' comes from a song that was popular in the British Isles in the early 1890s, called 'The Bogey Man' (later known as 'The Colonel Bogey March'). The title character of the song was an elusive figure who hid in the shadows: 'I'm the Bogey Man, catch me if you can.'

Golfers in Scotland and England equated the quest for the elusive Bogey Man with the quest for the elusive perfect score. By the mid to late 1890s, the term 'bogey score' referred to the ideal score a good player could be expected to make on a hole under perfect conditions. It also came to be used to describe stroke-play tournaments. Thus, in early rules books, we find a section detailing the regulations for 'bogey competitions'.
SOURCE: USGA

Rory's Fourth Major

Ninety-First PGA Championship, 13–16 August 2009
Hazeltine National Golf Club, Chaska, Minnesota

Rory put in an impressive performance at this tournament and was hard on the heels of his hero Tiger Woods. But it was South Korea's Yang Yong-eun (more commonly referred to as Y.E. Yang in the US) who outplayed the new kid on the block by winning three strokes over four-time champion Tiger. It was the first time Woods had failed to win a major he had led after 54 holes. Nonetheless, Rory tied with Lee Westwood for a highly respectable third place with –3.

Rory plays a bunker shot on the thirteenth hole during the third round of the ninety-first PGA Championship at Hazeltine National Golf Club, Minnesota on 15 August 2009.
JAMIE SQUIRE/GETTY IMAGES

Vivendi Trophy with Seve Ballesteros, 24–27 September 2009
Golf de Saint-Nom-la-Bretèche, Yvelines, France (European Tour)

This was the first edition of the **Seve Trophy**, listed on the European Tour schedule, and it took place with two experienced captains, selected by **Ryder Cup** captain Colin Montgomerie. Denmark's Thomas Bjørn led the Continental Europe team, whilst Irishman Paul McGinley skippered the ten players from Great Britain and Ireland.

Great Britain and Ireland quickly took an insurmountable 15–7 lead with seven singles matches remaining, after Rory defeated Henrik Stenson by one hole and Graeme McDowell beat Robert Karlsson. Britain and Ireland went on to win the trophy for a fifth consecutive time after beating Continental Europe 16½–11½ following the final ten singles matches.

Seve Trophy
The **Seve Trophy** was first played in 2000. It pits top European golfers against each other in a team-based competition, with a format similar to the **Ryder Cup**, with a few differences. First, the **Seve Trophy** is played over four days, not three. It also introduces the greensome, which does not exist in the **Ryder Cup**. The two teams of ten players representing Continental Europe or Great Britain and Ireland compete over four days, with five fourballs on the first two days, four greensomes on the next morning, four foursomes in the afternoon and ten singles on the final day. A total of 28 points are awarded, with 14½ needed to win.

Alfred Dunhill Links Championship, 1–4 October 2009
Old Course, St Andrews, Kingsbarns and Carnoustie, Fifeshire, Scotland

This tournament was played in a pro-am format over three courses in Fifeshire, namely **St Andrews**, **Kingsbarns** and **Carnoustie**.

Rory shared the lead with fellow Northern Irishman Michael Hoey and Scotland's Richie Ramsay after 36 holes. At just 20 years old, Rory added a superb second round of 65 at **St Andrews** to follow an opening round of 68 at **Carnoustie**. But Simon Dyson seized the initiative with six birdies in the first seven holes on his way to a 6-under-par 66 and a 20-under-par 268 total. He won by three strokes over Rory and Oliver Wilson. Rory had to be content with climbing to the top of Europe's money list (the Race to Dubai) with a joint runner-up finish of –17.

Rory reacts to his approach shot on the 13th hole during the final round of the UBS Hong Kong Open, 15 November 2009.
STUART FRANKLIN/GETTY

UBS Hong Kong Open, 12–15 November 2009
Hong Kong Golf Club, Fanling, Hong Kong

First held in 1959, the **UBS Hong Kong Open** is Hong Kong's oldest professional sporting event and is considered one of the jewels in the crown of Asian golf. It has always been staged at the same venue – the historic **Hong Kong Golf Club** – and is sanctioned by both the European and Asian Tours. Considered by many as Asia's Heritage tournament, the **UBS Hong Kong Open** is one of the biggest and most prestigious golf championships in the region. The tournament has formed part of the European PGA Tour since 2001 and attracts some of the world's best golfers.

Rory opened the 2009 European Tour with four top-five finishes in his first six starts, including his first win. And he closed it with seven finishes inside the top seven in his last eight starts. One of those was a runner-up finish at the **UBS Hong Kong Open**, the penultimate tournament on the European Tour schedule. That sent Rory into the final tournament – the **Dubai World Championship** – with a chance to win the European Tour money list title.

PGA Tour

The PGA Tour is a tax-exempt membership organisation of professional golfers. The mission of the PGA Tour is to expand domestically and internationally to substantially increase player financial benefits while maintaining its commitment to the integrity of the game. PGA Tour events are also committed to generating revenue for charitable causes in their communities. There are several funds available to provide financial assistance to poor and/or distressed members of the golf community through affiliates of the PGA Tour. These include the Professional Caddies Assistance Foundation, the Champions Tour Benevolent Fund and various charitable education funds.

Rory plays his second shot at the eighth hole during the final round of the
Dubai World Championship on the Earth Course, Jumeirah Golf Estates,
Dubai, 22 November 2009.
DAVID CANNON/GETTY IMAGES

Dubai World Championship Presented by DP World, 19–22 November 2009
Earth Course, Jumeirah Golf Estates, Dubai

The very first **Dubai World Championship** was held on the stunning **Earth Course** at **Jumeirah Golf Estates**. The world's best golfers competed for a staggering US $7.5 million in prize money on pristine greens. The championship is the culmination of the Race to Dubai, the season-long competition that replaced the European Tour's Order of Merit at the beginning of the 2008–09 schedule. It encompasses the Tour's most prestigious tournaments, the major championships and the **World Golf Championships**.

The top 60 players teed off over four days with no cut on the spectacular course designed by Greg Norman. Over 60,000 eager spectators poured onto the **Earth Course** to watch an enthralling four days of golf. Rory finished third with a score of 15 below par. It was the Englishman Lee Westwood who claimed victory in the inaugural event. But Rory would be back to claim his own title here in 2012.

As Rory finished an exciting 2009 season, he ranked second in the Race to Dubai behind Lee Westwood. By November, he had entered the top ten of the world rankings for the first time, in ninth place. Looking to the year ahead, he announced he would join the US-based PGA Tour for the 2010 season.

Race to Dubai

In 2009, the European Tour's Order of Merit was replaced by the Race To Dubai, with a bonus sum of $7.5 million (originally $10 million) to be distributed among the top 15 players at the end of the season. The new name reflected the addition of a new final tournament, the **Dubai World Championship**. This tournament is contested by the leading 60 players in the race following the season's penultimate event – the **UBS Hong Kong Open**. The winner of the Race To Dubai also receives a ten-year European Tour exemption, while the winner of the **Dubai World Championship** receives a five-year European Tour exemption.

Rory competes during the third round of the
€1.5 million Abu Dhabi HSBC Golf Championship
on 23 January 2010 in the Emirati capital.
AFP/GETTY IMAGES

Abu Dhabi HSBC Golf Championship, 21–24 January 2010
Abu Dhabi Golf Club, United Arab Emirates

Early in the new year, Rory took on the **Abu Dhabi HSBC Golf Championship**, a tournament on the European Tour schedule that has been played since 2006. It is typically the first of several consecutive weeks of European Tour play in the Persian Gulf during the early part of the schedule. The **Abu Dhabi HSBC Golf Championship** trophy is easily recognisable and, some would argue, one of the most stylish in golf. Known as the Falcon Trophy, it shows a falcon alighting on (or perhaps taking flight from or with) a golf ball. The tournament has been played at the same course in each year of its existence, on a majestic carpet of green surrounded by desert. It is a par-72 course.

Germany's Martin Kaymer won the second **Abu Dhabi HSBC Golf Championship** of his career following his victory two years earlier, edging out Englishman Ian Poulter after a final-round score of 66. Rory finished in third place with an impressive score of 269 –19.

Omega Dubai Desert Classic, 2 February 2010
Majlis Course, Emirates Golf Club, Dubai, United Arab Emirates

Rory returned to the **Omega Dubai Desert Classic** to defend his spectacular maiden victory of the previous year, but success eluded him as the Spanish player Miguel Ángel Jiménez secured first prize. Rory produced a valiant defence, but his one-over-par 73 was not enough to wipe out a two-shot overnight deficit. Rory finished in sixth place.

'I didn't play well,' Rory said. 'I didn't take my chances and it was just a bit of a struggle. I want to win and didn't even put myself in a position to do that. I didn't really get anything going.'

Nonetheless, the result meant that Rory had finished in the top seven in eight of his last nine events, dating back to August's 2009 **PGA Championship**.

Don'ts for Golfers

'Don't lose an opportunity of playing a round with a good player. You'll learn much more from losing holes to a superior player than from winning them from someone inferior to yourself.' (Sandy Green, *Don'ts for Golfers*, 1926)

Rory during the par-three challenge match on 2 February 2010, a preview for
the 2010 Omega Dubai Desert Classic on the Majlis Course at the incredible
Emirates Golf Club

DAVID CANNON/GETTY IMAGES EUROPE

Back Injury

Rory stepped up his training but, with a gruelling practice schedule often involving eight-hour sessions, he developed a back injury.

'I'm strapped pretty good. I've had the problem for a while, and it's just when I undertake a lot of practice. I've been out in the Middle East for four weeks so I think it's a repetitive injury and comes from hitting a lot of balls, and it just niggles a little bit.'

Despite the pain, Rory was still able to maintain his recent run of top-ten finishes and win sixth place at the **Omega Dubai Desert Classic**, which pushed the golf ace to a career-high world ranking. He took out a US PGA Tour card for the first time in the 2010 season and went on to a play at the **WGC – Accenture Match Play Championship** in Arizona on 17–21 February.

The **WGC – Accenture Match Play Championship** is one of the annual world golf championships. It is a knockout event generally staged late in February at the **Ritz-Carlton Golf Club**, Marana, Arizona. Rory got off to a good start, beating Kevin Na in the first round, but then lost in a tense playoff hole to Oliver Wilson.

After a two-week break he returned in the 2010 **Honda Classic** and finished in a tie for fortieth place.

Surrounded by giant cacti, Rory hits to the second green during the second round of the WGC – Accenture Match Play Championship at the Ritz-Carlton Golf Club in Arizona on 18 February 2010.
STAN BADZ/PGA TOUR

Masters Tournament, 8–11 April 2010
Augusta National Golf Club, Augusta, Georgia, USA

Rory and Graeme McDowell of Northern Ireland with Thongchai Jaidee of Thailand walk off a tee box during a practice round prior to the 2010 Masters Tournament at Augusta National Golf Club on 6 April 2010.

JAMIE SQUIRE/GETTY IMAGES

If Rory wanted to become the youngest **Masters Tournament** champion in history – a position currently held by Tiger Woods, of course – he had to do it at the 2010 tournament. Just four weeks later he would be 21.

For many, based on his recent form, the odds on Rory donning a green jacket were getting longer and longer. But Rory believed he was putting his game back together and there is no more inspiring stage than **Augusta National Golf Club**.

'I feel I'm now playing well enough to be in contention. I feel like the shots are there again. I'm hitting a lot of fairways and my distance is up again. I'm certainly moving in the right direction. My confidence wasn't great a month ago, but it's probably back close to seven or eight. And I love this golf course.'

But the 20-year-old shot 77 and missed the cut, a year after finishing twentieth on his Augusta debut. Now, with a niggling back injury causing more mental than physical problems, Rory decided to take a six-week sabbatical in order to conquer his problems.

'I just didn't play well and I need a bit of time to get back on track,' he said. 'I don't know what is going on. I just need to take a bit of a break and come back with a refreshed attitude. I am getting frustrated very easily and getting down on myself. I just think that I need to go home and get my head sorted. I am supposed to play Quail Hollow [on the US Tour] in a couple of weeks, but I might need a bit more time.'

Of course Rory did manage to play the **Quail Hollow Championship** – with brilliant results.

'The confidence to pull off a tough shot just comes with practice. Golf is probably more mental than physical. You know, everyone has to learn and develop and the best way to do that is by learning from your mistakes.'

Rory, Facebook interview with Augdemars Piguet

Rory makes a birdie during the Quail Hollow Championship on 2 May 2010 in Charlotte, North Carolina. That competition was his first PGA Tour win.
STREETER LECKA/GETTY IMAGES

Critics agree that 'sensational' was the only word to describe Rory's golf that day at the **Quail Hollow Club**. It was the best he had ever played as a professional and millions watched on television. He finished a staggering 15 under par. It was his first triumph on the PGA Tour, at the tender age of 20.

Here was evidence before the world of the genius of this much-talked-about youngster from Holywood. Not one to forget his Northern Ireland roots, Rory came home to take on more challenges and support his hero Sir Nick Faldo in a new golfing challenge.

You can't beat the setting. A private 600-acre peninsula between Lower Lough Erne and Castle Hume Lough. Lough Erne Golf Club poses a really tough challenge and the resort as a whole has some of the best facilities in Northern Ireland.

He made all the birdies. I was just out there for the ride. Darren Clarke

In July 2010, paired with Darren Clarke for the first time in competition, the superior display by Rory at **Lough Erne Resort** was more than enough to see off the challenge from Pádraig Harrington and Shane Lowry.

The Northern Ireland pair proved to be a solid combination as they beat their southern Ireland counterparts by a single shot, six under to five under.

By October in the same year, Rory had earned a coveted spot in the **Ryder Cup** team.

Rory jokes with Darren Clarke as they prepare to tee off at the Lough Erne Resort.
CHARLES McQUILLAN/PACEMAKER

The **Faldo Championship Course** at **Lough Erne Resort** in Enniskillen, County Fermanagh (7,167 yards, par 72) was designed by six-time major winner Sir Nick Faldo. It was the first golf course he designed on the island of Ireland. The course is considered one of the top 100 in the world by many golf experts. It provides golfers with superb year-round playing conditions as well as breathtaking views of the Fermanagh lakelands.

Rory with Sir Nick Faldo
RUSSELL LOUGH ERNE RESORT

(Left–right) Martin Kaymer, Rory, caddy John McLaren and Graeme McDowell of the European Ryder Cup team pose with Rory wigs during a practice round on 29 September 2010 prior to the 2010 Ryder Cup at the Celtic Manor Resort, Wales.
ANDREW REDINGTON/GETTY IMAGES

Ryder Cup Hero

Rory was one of a 12-strong team skippered by Colin Montgomerie when the European **Ryder Cup** team faced the USA at **Celtic Manor Resort** in Wales. Rory's partner in the pairs was one of his best friends, fellow Northern Irishman Graeme McDowell. Rory said it was 'great to play with one of [his] best friends'.

After securing a half point against Stewart Cink and winning the **Ryder Cup**, Rory glowed with team pride.

'I truly believe this is the best tournament in the world,' he said.

Rory tees off during a practice round on 29 September 2010 prior to the 2010 Ryder Cup at the Celtic Manor Resort, Wales.
ROSS KINNAIRD/GETTY IMAGES

History of the Ryder Cup

Samuel Ryder was an English sea merchant and entrepreneur from St Albans, who had made his fortune from selling penny packets of seeds. He took up golf late in life to improve his health and enlisted Abe Mitchell as his personal tutor. Ryder was so fascinated to see Mitchell and George Duncan defeat defending **Open Tournament** champion Jim Barnes and Walter Hagan at Wentworth in 1926 that he was heard to say in the nineteenth hole, 'We must do this again.' Ryder donated a gold cup worth £250 as part of the prize and the golfing figure at the top of the trophy stands as a lasting memorial to Abe Mitchell. So it was that one of the world's greatest sporting events was born.

ROSS KINNAIRD/GETTY IMAGES

HOLE	1	2	3	4	5	6	7	8	9	10	11	12	13	14	15	16	17	18
PAR	4	5	4	3	4	3	4	5	4	4	4	3	5	4	5	3	4	4

LEADERS

11	McILROY	1	1	1	1	1	10	10											
8	CABRERA	8	9	8	8	8	8												
8	SCHWARTZEL	9	9	11	10	10	8												
8	CHOI	8	8	8	8	8	8												
8	DAY	7	8	8	8	8	8												
7	SCOTT	7	8	8	7	7	8												
7	DONALD	7	8	8	8	8	8												
5	WOODS	5	6	7	6	6	7	8	10										
5	FISHER	5	6	6	5	5	5	6											
3	WESTWOOD	3	4	1	4	4	5	6											

THRU 6

McILROY	10
CABRERA	8

Rory hits his approach shot to the seventh green as his caddy J.P. Fitzgerald looks on during the final round of the 2011 Masters Tournament at Augusta National Golf Club (April 10) in Augusta, Georgia.
HARRY HOW/GETTY IMAGES

For Rory, 2010 had been a highly rewarding year, as he gained more experience on the professional circuits. And his star was still rising. He had achieved sixth place at the **UBS Hong Kong Open** (18–21 November 2010) and moved his game up a gear to attain fifth place in the **Dubai World Championship Presented by DP World** (25–28 November 2010). By December 2010, he was chasing pole position and bagged fourth place at the **Chevron World Challenge** at **Sherwood Country Club**, Thousand Oaks, California (2–5 December 2010).

But 2011 was to bring fresh challenges. At the start of the year, Rory finished in second place at the **Abu Dhabi HSBC Golf Championship** (20–23 January 2011). Yet, after a poor seventeenth-place finish at the **Honda Classic** on the **Championship Course, PGA National Golf Club**, Palm Beach Gardens, Florida (3–6 March), Rory appeared out of sorts. His play rallied at the **WGC – Cadillac Championship** on the **TPC Blue Monster Course, Doral Golf Resort and Spa**, Miami, Florida (10–13 March), where he finished tenth.

But the much-anticipated US Masters was to cast the largest shadow over of any previous lack of form. In April, Rory took part in the **Masters Tournament** at **Augusta National Golf Club** in Georgia and got off to a cracking pace. Three rounds in he was leading – the youngest player to do so since Seve Ballesteros, who was 23 when he led in 1980.

But against all expectations, Rory's game deteriorated rapidly in the final round. At the tenth hole, he hooked his drive, clipped a tree and ricocheted into the garden of a neighbouring house. He ended up with a triple-bogey seven. He had begun the day with a four-stroke lead but ended it ten strokes behind the victor, Charl Schwartzel, finishing an unexpected fifteenth. It was a devastating blow.

For Rory, it was time to regroup, re-evaluate his game and the fallout. He was keen to put the matter into context:

> 'I'm very disappointed and will be for the next few days, but I've got to take the positives out of this week. I led the tournament for 63 holes and that will build a bit of character in me.'

Rory leaves the 18th hole green after finishing the final round with a final score of four under par at the 2011 Masters Tournament at Augusta National Golf Club (April 10th) in Augusta, Georgia.
ROBYN BECK/AFP/GETTY IMAGES

Rory decided simply to move on from his infamous 'Masters meltdown', as the world's media were calling it. After such a high-profile tournament, it was remarkable that he managed to hold his nerve in the public arena at all. He did so, however, to finish in a solid third place at the **Maybank Malaysian Open** in Kuala Lumpur on 14–17 April 2011.

But Rory's form remained irregular. He went on to miss the cut at the **Wells Fargo Championship** at the **Quail Hollow Club** in North Carolina, USA, on 5–8 May 2011. It was time to reassess matters. Besides, there were other demands on Rory's time that were to prove more rewarding than he could have ever imagined.

Rory reacts with disappointment during the 75th Masters Tournament at Augusta National Golf Club in Augusta, 10 April, 2011.
TIM DOMINICK/THE STATE/MCT VIA GETTY IMAGES

There are a lot worse things that can happen in your life. Rory

Haiti has made me realise there is more to life than golf. It has instilled in me a feeling that, the next time I struggle on the golf course or whatever, I'll think of the people of Haiti. That will change my mindset pretty quickly.

Rory

In 2011, Rory was appointed a national ambassador for UNICEF Ireland. He made his first official humanitarian trip in June that year, visiting newly built schools, a maternity centre and camps for displaced people in Haiti, just a year after an earthquake devastated the Caribbean nation.

Joining UNICEF and meeting the children of Haiti a couple of months before the **US Open Championship** had a powerful effect upon him.

As a UNICEF ambassador, Rory helped to raise funds and create a broader knowledge and awareness of the issues surrounding children's rights and welfare.

Rory is a great asset. Being young and successful, he is a perfect fit for UNICEF. Given his international profile, he will help us to draw attention to the needs of the vulnerable children we work with. UNICEF Ireland , 2011

A kid grows up a lot faster on the golf course. Golf teaches you how to behave. Jack Nicklaus

Style with Content

Rory decided to turn the worldwide interest in his personal style and sponsored equipment to another project very close to his heart. On 10 January, he announced he had started a new charity, the **Rory Foundation**. The foundation's first project was to promote awareness of the suffering of children by putting the name of chosen charities on his bag whenever possible.

'When I was younger my parents sacrificed everything to allow me to play the game I love. Having that support from my family gave me the opportunity to chase my dreams. But I know that every child is not so fortunate. My aim is that the **Rory Foundation** will support childrens' charities big and small, around the world, which are trying to give kids that helping hand.'

Rory with seven-year-old James Bannatyne and his new golf bag, branded with the Northern Ireland Cancer Fund for Children logo, part of the Rory Foundation charity initiative, during practice for the Abu Dhabi HSBC Golf Championship at Abu Dhabi Golf Club on 15 January 2013.
ANDREW REDINGTON/GETTY IMAGES

Rory began with the **6 Bags Project**, in which he displayed the name of a children's charity in each of the first six tournaments he played. During each tournament, the bag was auctioned through www.roryfoundation.com and the proceeds given to that charity.

The **Northern Ireland Cancer Fund for Children** was featured on the bag at his first tournament, the **Abu Dhabi HSBC Golf Championship**, on 17–20 January 2013.

Rory with five-year-old Ben Bingham, who had a kidney transplant at the Royal Belfast Hospital for Sick Children, supporting the Cool FM Cash for Kids Radiothon, which raised money for the hospital.
COLM O'REILLY/PACEMAKER PRESS

It is repetition of affirmations that leads to belief – and once that belief becomes a deep conviction, things begin to happen.

After the Masters, Rory posted this message, quoting the great Muhammad Ali.

Back in the Game

After his trip to Haiti, Rory knew that he had to put his game into context. It was time to relax and rediscover that joy in the game of golf that had brought him so far.

In June that same year, Rory was ready to step up to the **US Open Championship** at the **Congressional Country Club** in Bethesda, Maryland. As many golfers know, this is an unforgiving course, with unique characteristics that challenge even the finest of players.

Legend in the making: Rory celebrates with caddy J.P. Fitzgerald after his tee shot on the tenth hole *en route* to his record-breaking victory in the US Open in June 2011.

EPA

Rory reaffirmed his self-belief and played enthralling golf. He tore apart the reputation of the tough **US Open**. After Augusta and the US **Masters Tournament**, he didn't take anything for granted. At the par-three tenth hole, Rory played an incredible iron shot. Ultimately, he finished a whopping 16 under par, shattering course records. He had destroyed a world-class field of professionals on his way to an eight-shot clear victory.

Happy Father's Day, Dad. This one's for you.

His father Gerry raced out onto the green at the eighteenth as Rory won. At 22, he became the youngest man to win the **US Open Championship** since Bobby Jones in 1923.

ANDREW GOMBERT EPA

Rory set 11 **US Open Championship** records that weekend, including the lowest total 72-hole score (268) and the lowest total under par (–16). Rory and fellow golfer Robert Garrigus became the fifth and sixth golfers in the history of the championship to score under par in all four rounds.

It was the second straight **US Open Championship** title for Northern Ireland. Defending champion Graeme McDowell walked back across the bridge to the eighteenth green to embrace the new winner.

'You're a legend,' McDowell told him.

A replica of the US Open trophy in Holywood Golf Club's Rory Trophy Room

Graeme McDowell was waiting by the eighteenth green at Congressional to offer congratulations after Rory kept the Open trophy for Northern Ireland.
ANDREW GOMBERT/EPA

77

I'm so proud to be from here. I've won this **US Open** trophy but I'd just like you to know that it belongs to all of you. Rory

Rory travelled home to Holywood Golf Club, where it had all begun for him. Holywood fans turned out in force at George Best Belfast City Airport. At the entrance to the town of Holywood, a roadside banner of congratulations caught his attention. Fans swamped the golf club. The town's disappointment at his final-round fall in the **Masters Tournament** in April was forgotten and Holywood locals rejoiced at his win.

Fans and members at Holywood Golf Club react to Rory's win.
ALAN LEWIS

'I asked Rory after he won the **US Open** how he felt when he was six shots clear – did he feel nervous? Rory just said he was more nervous in the third round because he wanted to get himself into the lead. When he got that lead, he felt all the hard work had been done. In the last round he said he felt fine and he had learned from the US **Masters** how to handle himself. That is one of Rory's gifts. He has the ability to learn from where he goes wrong. That is what makes him a champion. It is how you respond from failure. A lot of us can't do it. He can deal with it.'

Michael Eaton, HGC captain, March 2012–March 2013

Rory being sprayed w
champagne wh
holding the US Op
trophy dur
celebrations
Holywood Golf Cl
Northern Irela
ALAN L

Northern Ireland: 'It really is a small wee place here and we are talking about one of the greatest players ever in the world.'

Michael Eaton, HGC captain, March 2012–March 2013

The win made Rory an international superstar. Demands were made of him for press and television appearances as he rubbed shoulders with the rich and famous.

Staying grounded has always been Rory's style and he was applauded for the contribution he had made to golf in Northern Ireland. The win meant that, in a poll conducted a few days later, 39 per cent of British 18-to-24-year-olds said they had been inspired to try golf for the first time because of Rory. He was named by *Golf Club Management* magazine as the second most powerful person in British golf.

Rory has had to learn to cope with constant demands from press and public alike.
PACEMAKER PRESS

Twenty-two-year-old Rory meets Northern Ireland's first minister, Peter Robinson, and deputy first minister, Martin McGuinness, at Stormont Castle on 30 June 2011.
KELVIN BOYES/PRESS EYE

NIPHO/LORRAINE O'SULLIVAN

With his star still rising, later that month Rory met Ireland's taoiseach, Enda Kenny, when he took part in the 2011 **Irish Open** pro-am tournament at **Killarney Golf and Fishing Club**, County Kerry, on 27 July 2011.

With his personality, everybody loves him. People expect a lot of him and it's very difficult. Michael Bannon

Rory waits with his golf bag after injuring his wrist during the first round of the ninety-third PGA Championship at the Atlanta Athletic Club in Johns Creek, Georgia on 11 August 2011.
DAVID CANNON/GETTY IMAGES

Rory took a month off from competitive golf and didn't touch a golf club for ten days after the **US Open Championship**. After that he just hit balls on the range.

Rory then resumed his schedule, but at the British **Open Championship** at **Royal St George's Golf Club**, Sandwich, Kent (14–17 July), he struggled in tough weather over a difficult layout.

Worse was to come at the **PGA Championship** at the **Atlanta Athletic Club**, Johns Creek, Georgia on 11–14 August. Rory injured his wrist on the third hole of the first round after attempting to play a stroke from behind a tree root. There was concern that his professional career had been seriously cut short.

Thankfully, Rory made a quick recovery and found himself cool under pressure as he travelled to the Far East to compete for the prestigious **Lake Malaren Shanghai Masters**.

Shining under pressure

Something that I feel I can still get better at is winning, and putting myself in the position to win when I'm not playing my best. Rory

Rory celebrates his win after finishing at 18 under par and defeating Anthony Kim of the US in a playoff on the final day of the Lake Malaren Shanghai Masters golf tournament on 30 October 2011.

MARK RALSTON/AFP/GETTY IMAGES

Did You Know?

The **Shanghai Masters** has the biggest first prize in golf at $2 million (£1.3 million), with the runner-up receiving $750,000 (£488,000) from a total prize pot of $5 million (£3.25 million).

In a sudden-death playoff against Anthony Kim of the US, Rory's performance at the **Lake Malaren Shanghai Masters** proved dramatic, to say the least. His final round turned into an unexpected battle to claim one of the biggest prizes in golf. Rory struggled to stay on form. But despite the pressure he held his nerve and claimed yet another victory.

To be a champion you must act like one. Sir Henry Cotton

WGC – HSBC Champions, 3–6 November 2011
Shenshan Golf Club, Shanghai, China

(Left–right) Adam Scott of Australia, Lee Westwood of England, Francesco Molinari of Italy, Rory and Keegan Bradley of the USA take part in a traditional Chinese dragon dance at the Peninsula Hotel on 1 November 2011, to herald the start of the WGC – HSBC Champions in Shanghai, China.
ANDREW REDINGTON/GETTY IMAGES

2011 proved to be Rory's year. To cap it all, the win that had eluded him just three years earlier was his. He was victorious in the UBS Hong Kong Open in the Race to Dubai in December 2011.

Rory greets marshalls after winning the UBS Hong Kong Open at the Hong Kong Golf Club, Fanling on 4 December 2011.
STUART FRANKLIN/GETTY IMAGES

In the New Year Honours list for 2012, Rory and close friend Darren Clarke received awards for their 2011 successes and services to sport. Darren became an OBE, while Rory was appointed an MBE for his **US Open Championship** win in June 2011. Rory was 'humbled' to be on the list and said:

'Many people on the honours list have made huge personal sacrifices and contributed significantly to society during their lives. I feel very fortunate to be in their company.'

The question on everyone's lips has always been, 'What is it that makes Rory so special?'

Holywood Golf Club general manager Paul Gray has seen Rory play since he was a small child and watched his game develop for over 20 years.

'You need a spark of genius and 100 per cent passion to be able to sustain success. It's all about patience, perseverance and practice – putting the hours in – disciplined hours of really training yourself to do what you want to do. Rory certainly did that. When Rory used to go to the driving range, I would be down there teaching or practising myself. Obviously, as a professional, I had reached a certain level. I would hit a bucket of balls or perhaps two to keep that level up. But there was Rory, at 11 or 12 years of age, walking down the range with two full buckets in his hands and his father Gerry behind him carrying another two full buckets. As a professional, I thought I practised hard, but I saw this kid hitting four buckets of balls day in, day out. On reflection, that puts his genius into perspective for me.'

Fitness Advisor Steve McGregor

Rory's posture and physique changed greatly under the direction of Steve McGregor, Ph.D. Much in demand, the British trainer also oversees the fitness regime of Lee Westwood and is a consultant with a number of professional teams, including Manchester City and the New York Knicks.

'I've worked with a physio before, but no one of Steve's calibre and experience. I know from his work with Lee how beneficial he could be in building up my body. If my work with him makes a fraction of a difference, then it will be worth it.'

McGregor confirmed, 'Rory works out five times per week, 90 minutes per day. We don't give [regimen] specifics – he sees his fitness as part of his competitive advantage. But we train indoors, outdoors, with weights, on the treadmill, doing sprints, and he swims when he's near the beach.'

I feel a lot more stable in my golf swing. There's a lot less moving parts. Rory

'The benefits? His clubhead speed has increased, He's driving it longer. He can hit it harder without losing balance. He looks more stable in his swing, and he's getting more yardage with less effort.' We've added muscle mass. Rory weighed 160 pounds [in 2010] and is now 170. That's a 20-pound change in muscle composition, when you take into account loss of body fat. And he's not done. He's not where he wants to be. He sees himself as a golfer and an athlete. We're talking about getting to 175 pounds or more. Why? When you increase muscle mass, you're going to be hitting shorter irons into greens.'

'It's important to vary your workout, to stay fresh but also not to overuse certain muscles. We vary his workout every 6 to 8 weeks. Everything we do relates to his golf. Our goal is to keep him physically robust, so that his body can stand up to hitting all those shots, and so that he can practice as much as he wants.'

Connell Barrett, interview with Steve McGregor for GOLF Magazine, December 2012

You must work very hard to become a natural golfer. Gary Player

I was almost born with a golf club in my hand. I remember videos and pictures of me with a plastic club, hitting balls inside and outside the house. From a very early age I have been in love with the game. Rory

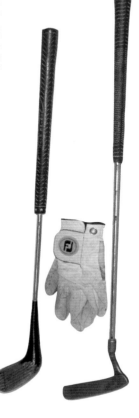

Rory's first clubs
PRIVATE FAMILY COLLECTION

The most common grip among professional golfers is the overlapping or 'Vardon' grip. Harry Vardon popularised this grip in the early years of the twentieth century. This grip is the one most likely to be taught by golf instructors.

However, some notable golfers have used the interlocking grip – like Rory. In the interlocking grip for right-handed players, the little finger of the right hand hooks around the forefinger of the left hand. This forms a physical connection that pulls the two hands tightly together. When hands in this position wrap around a club's cushioned grip, the result is an extremely strong 'joint'. This physical strength is the big advantage of an interlocking grip and its benefits manifest themselves in a variety of ways.

Harry Vardon, Francis Ouimet and Ted Ray, after Ouimet's victory at the US Open in 1913
OUIMET FOUNDATION

Rory's grip
SCOTT HALLERAN/GETTY IMAGES

One advantage of the Vardon overlapping grip is that it suits larger hands. It is considered by many pros as a way to unify the hands.

A disadvantage of the overlapping grip is that, for people with small hands, the right hand can tend to be too far under or over the club.

Early Clubs

When golf was first played on the east coast of Scotland in 1457, the players used their own carved clubs and balls. However, it was not long before golf enthusiasts of the fifteenth century approached skilled craftsmen to make them sets of clubs.

Don'ts for Golfers

'Don't blame your clubs for faults of your own if you analyse your methods of using the implements. If, after careful testing, a club continues to disappoint you try using a different one.' (Sandy Green, *Don'ts for Golfers*, 1926)

Rory has had a rather distinctive putting grip since his amateur days – middle, ring and little fingers of the right hand wrapped around the left and facing the target. But since his 2011 'Masters meltdown', he has been working with noted short-game expert Dave Stockton, who has tweaked Rory's putting stroke using a new grip. When putting, all the fingers of his right hand now rest on the shaft, with the left index finger positioned on top of the ring and middle fingers of the right hand.

Rory using the interlocking grip

Putting Coach Dave Stockton

After letting victory slip away in the 2011 **Masters Tournament**, Rory turned to Dave Stockton, who captained the victorious 1991 USA **Ryder Cup** team. Stockton urged Rory to forget about the mechanics and revert to his natural feel. The improvement was stunning. Stockton spent less than 15 minutes working with Rory at the **Quail Hollow Championship** and a month later Rory bounced back to capture the **US Open Champtionship**.

Rory has said that, in the wake of his historic triumph at the US **PGA Championship** in August 2012, Stockton simply said to him:

'Just go out and play with a smile on your face. Enjoy it. This is what you've always wanted to do since you were a little boy. There's no point in getting frustrated out there or getting upset. Just go out and enjoy it.'

'Getting the line and ball right and rolling them in on the putting green – Rory can do that now. He used to just thump them in years ago, a bit like Tiger Woods did in his early days. That's all changed now. Dave Stockton has given him confidence in his putting.'

Michael Eaton, HGC captain, March 2012–March 2013

Rory and putting coach Dave Stockton stand on the practice range on 3 April 2012, during a practice round prior to the start of the 2012 Masters Tournament at Augusta National Golf Club.

I stand up, look at the shot, assess it, know the shot I'm going to hit and hit it … I think my short routine is okay … I have a couple of practice swings, visualise the shot, feel it, see it, do it and let it go … there's no point taking time over things as you just confuse yourself … Rory

I would like the player to own his own game, own his own swing, and I'm there to make sure it's right. But it's not my swing – it's Rory's swing. It's his game. I think that's very important – that he has control over that. That's why I don't have to be there all the time. He works it out for himself.

Rory had a great swing at 14, 15, 16. You don't actually change that swing; you just check to see if it's in the right position. You know you don't go changing that. Why would you want to?

They talk about Rory's flexibility now and how he turns his right shoulder to the target. But he was doing it even then. You see the control he has over the ball for such a young fellow. I didn't teach him to play golf; I just taught him how to swing the club. As I always say to Rory, 'The rest is up to you.'

Michael Bannon GOLF *Magazine*

Rory's swing technique, aged 19, as he plays a shot on the fourth hole during the Dubai Desert Classic tournament on 31 January 2009
MARWAN NAAMANI/AFP/GETTY IMAGES

Swing Coach Michael Bannon

Bannon continued to work with Rory throughout his teens and beyond. Bannon was the first to identify him as a potential world number one. In October 2012, Rory persuaded Bannon to reduce his club professional commitments and become his dedicated coach.

I've been with Michael since I was seven or eight years old. He's a friend of my dad's and was the professional at his club. And as I was starting to play the game, that's how we got together. That was at Holywood Golf Club, where I'm still a member. Michael moved on to nearby Bangor Golf Club but I continued to go to him for lessons.

Fast forward a dozen years or so, and one of the hottest properties in the game is still working with the same coach. Most golfers who play on the world stage pass through a succession of trainers *en route* to the top. Rory is almost unique in that he has been with his original coach since day one.

Rory talks with Michael during the pro-am tournament at the Honda Classic at PGA National Golf Club, Palm Beach Gardens, Florida, on 27 February 2013.
STUART FRANKLIN/GETTY IMAGES

He's got me this far, so it's obviously working. There's no need to change anything or do anything differently. He's a really good teacher – he keeps things simple and never complicates them. And as well as being a brilliant coach, he's a very good player who understands the game. Rory

Golf is 20 per cent talent and 80 per cent management. Ben Hogan

In late October 2011, Rory parted company with long-time agent Andrew 'Chubby' Chandler to join Ryder Cup partner Graeme McDowell at the Dublin management company Horizon Sports Management. Rory had been represented by Chubby and International Sports Management since he had turned professional in September 2007.

'I am now keen to move onto the next stage of my career and I feel this will be facilitated by a fresh view and a new structure around me,' Rory said in a statement. ISM said it had taken 'great pride … in guiding him successfully through his formative years as a professional golfer'. Rory thanked Chandler for his 'guidance, representation and management', acknowledging that Chubby and his team had played a very important role in his success to date.

Rory and his former manager Andrew 'Chubby' Chandler during the pro-am event prior to the Johnnie Walker Championship at the Gleneagles Hotel and Resort in Perthshire, Scotland, on 27 August 2008
ROSS KINNAIRD/GETTY IMAGES

Rory found himself catapulted into a whole new sphere of sponsorship deals that would place him on the same stage as superstars David Beckham and Tiger Woods. Endorsements for Omega, Bose and – perhaps biggest of all – Nike, made global headline news.

Nike

In the latter half of 2012, Rory signed a historic sponsorship deal with Nike for an undisclosed figure, which was said to dwarf the pay scale of Nike stablemate Tiger Woods. Brokered by his new agents, the deal was made public to huge fanfare and global media attention at a press launch in Abu Dhabi on 14 January 2013.

Aside from the sheer spectacle surrounding the announcement, there was concern from amateurs and professionals alike that adapting to Nike clubs might prove no easy feat for Rory. Many golf commentators feared it might affect his play. As Rory's 2013 season got under way, he certainly struggled with his game and form. By mid-May 2013 the media was speculating that Rory had decided to break with Horizon Sports Management. Months later, on 27 September 2013 a statement was issued confirming that Rory had indeed set up his own management company, to be called Rory McIlroy Incorporated.

Significant though these management changes were, it was Rory's new sponsorship contract which really caught the public's imagination. Years of hard work had brought Rory into the spotlight as a genuine contender. Crowned by Nike, he was now standing on the shoulders of giants – an international icon – as a result of a truly momentous 2012 season.

A hologram projection of Rory McIlroy on water as he is unveiled as a new brand ambassador for Nike at Fairmont Bab Al Bahr Hotel in Abu Dhabi, United Arab Emirates, on 14 January 2013
MATTHEW LEWIS/GETTY IMAGES

The 2012 season was the one in which Rory truly established himself as Holywood's global superstar.

He won five times in 2012, including his second major title, the **PGA Championship**, in August. In November, at only 23 years old, he won the European Tour's Race to Dubai, finished second in the PGA Tour's **FedEx Cup Playoffs** and captured both the PGA Tour and European Tour money titles.

He became the fourth youngest US PGA champion of all time. It was the second major of his career.

I set a target to get to number one in the world this year and I achieved that. And then I had to sit back and reassess my goals, because that was the goal.

A view from the grandstand as Rory hits off the first tee during round three of the ninety-fourth PGA Championship at the Ocean Course at Kiawah Island Golf Resort, South Carolina, on 11 August 2012

ANDREW REDINGTON/GETTY IMAGES

A replica of the PGA Cup sits in Holywood Golf Club's Rory Trophy Room

DERMOTT DUNBAR

It's one thing to win, but another to wrap your arms around history.

Gene Wojciechowski, sports writer

Rory kisses the trophy on the beach on 12 August 2012, after winning the ninety-fourth PGA Championship at Kiawah Island, South Carolina.

DON EMMERT/AFP/GETTYIMAGES

I made it very clear I wasn't too happy with how I've performed in the majors since the US Open. I didn't really contend. And I came in [to the media centre] Wednesday and just talked about giving myself a chance and, to be honest, that's all I wanted to do.

Rory made these remarks after breaking the PGA record for the widest margin of victory, previously held by Jack Nicklaus, who won in 1980 by seven strokes.

It was an incredible day. I set myself a target that if I got to 12 under, no one was going to catch me. I went one better. To sit up here and see this trophy and call myself a multiple major champion ... I know I've talked about it in the past, and not many people have done it. I'm very privileged to join such an elite list of names.

Of course, no one is close to what Tiger Woods has accomplished in golf. He won 54 times and 10 majors before turning 30.

I've won my second major at the same age as Tiger, but he went on that incredible run and won so many. I'd love to sit here and tell you I'm going to do the same thing, but I just don't know. It's been great to win my first major and to back that up with another one. I can't ask for more.

Nonetheless, Rory did make PGA Championship history. Nobody – not even Jack Nicklaus or Tiger Woods – has ever won this championship by eight strokes. Rory's victory was so complete that he would have had to take a 12 on the final hole even to force a playoff.

This week I'm not the number-one player in the world. I'm one person in a 12-man team. Rory

The European team: (left–right) Peter Hanson, Ian Poulter, Martin Kaymer, Graeme McDowell, Rory McIlroy, Luke Donald, José María Olazábal (captain), Sergio García, Francesco Molinari, Lee Westwood, Paul Lawrie, Justin Rose and Nicolas Colsaerts pose for an official photograph on 25 September 2012, during the second preview day of the thirty-ninth Ryder Cup at Medinah Country Club near Chicago, Illinois.

ROSS KINNAIRD/GETTY IMAGES

'The most rewarding things you do in life are often the ones that look like they cannot be done.'

ARNOLD PALMER

Ryder Cup, 28–30 September 2012
Medinah Country Club, Medinah, Illinois

This will surely go down as one of the most extraordinary tournaments in **Ryder Cup** history. At the start of the final day's play, the US led 10–6 and required 4½ points to win; Europe required a virtually impossible 8 points to retain the cup and 8½ to win it outright.

The drama was heightened when Rory failed to arrive as expected for the final day. His European teammates started to worry. Two minutes late and he would forfeit the opening hole; five minutes late and he faced disqualification. European captain José María Olazábal admitted that his heart was 'racing quicker than expected' when his man failed to materialise. 'All of a sudden we realised Rory was not here.'

But with 11 minutes to go before the match started, Rory was driven into the parking lot in an unmarked police car. He raced across to the practice putting green and then proceeded to put in an incredible first nine holes. Rory revealed that his phone had been to blame for his late arrival.

I read the tee times on my phone, and they are obviously on Eastern Time and it's Central Time here. I was just casually walking out of my hotel room and got a phone call saying you've got 25 minutes until you tee off. I've never been so worried driving to the golf course. Luckily, there was a state trooper outside who gave me the escort here. If it wasn't for him, I wouldn't have got here in time. So I just ran into the clubhouse, got my shoes on and picked it up on the first tee.

Rory walks to the first tee after arriving late to the golf course during the singles matches for the thirty-ninth Ryder Cup at Medinah Country Club on 30 September 2012.
DAVID CANNON/GETTY IMAGES

Rory takes a bow, victorious after his match on the seventeenth hole during Sunday singles at Medinah Country Club on 30 September 2012.
KOHJIRO KINNO/SPORTS ILLUSTRATED/GETTY IMAGES

BELOW: Rory hits his tee shot on the fourteenth hole during the singles matches for the thirty-ninth Ryder Cup at Medinah Country Club near Chicago, Illinois, on 30 September 2012.

ANDY LYONS/GETTY IMAGES

Rory and Graeme McDowell during the afternoon four-ball matches for the thirty-ninth Ryder Cup at Medinah Country Club, Illinois, on 28 September 2012

ANDREW REDINGTON/GETTY IMAGES

Incredibly, Europe achieved one of the greatest comebacks in Ryder Cup history by winning eight and tying one of the 12 singles matches.

Rory, Darren Clarke and Sergio García celebrate. A massive clock is hung around Rory's neck to remind him to arrive on time in future.
DAVID CANNON/GETTY IMAGES

Rory went on to beat his individual opponent Keegan Bradley, as the European team came back after trailing by a seemingly hopeless four points overnight.

Don'ts for Golfers
'Don't "give" anything when you are playing for a team. If, when playing on your own, you care to be generous, that is entirely your own affair. But when playing for a team, you are not playing for yourself and the team expects you to WIN.' (Sandy Green, *Don'ts for Golfers*, 1926)

Rory and Tiger Woods of the USA greet each other on the eighteenth green after Europe defeated the USA 14½ to 13½ to retain the trophy in the thirty-ninth Ryder Cup on 30 Septembe 2012.
MIKE EHRMANN/GETTY IMAGES

99

Rory has had five wins in 2012 and his tenth pro-career win. I said to him at the start of the year: let's make it ten wins. I said, if you win ten we can move on towards winning twenty. That's one of our goals.   Michael Bannon

It's just a great way to end what has been a great year – my best season so far.

Rory poses with his trophy after winning the DP World Tour Championship, Dubai on 25 November 2012. Rory responded in magnificent fashion to Justin Rose's course-record round by making five birdies in his last five holes to win the title.

KARIM SAHIB/AFP/GETTY IMAGES

As if Rory needed to prove anything else as the 2012 season drew to a close, he signed out the year with five consecutive birdies to capture the **DP World Tour Championship, Dubai** title on 25 November 2012 at **Jumeirah Golf Estates**.

The 23-year-old finished with the flourish of a true champion, clinching victory by two strokes with a closing 66 and a 23-under tally of 265. Rory won the 2012 Race to Dubai with record earnings for a single season, emulating the 2011 winner, Luke Donald, by winning both the European and US PGA Tour money lists in the same season.

I just wanted to finish the season the way I think it deserved to be finished, Rory told journalists after winning for the fifth time in 2012.

He certainly did that. And, after winning his second major title at the ninety-fourth USA **PGA Championship** in August, he added three wins and another three top-ten finishes in eight events.

To cap it all, Rory was was named the PGA Tour Player of the Year by fellow players on the US Tour. He is the youngest to hold the title since Tiger Woods claimed it in 1997 at the age of 21.

Rory's achievements were acknowledged when he was also shortlisted for BBC Sports Personality of the Year 2012. In December he picked up the title of Northern Ireland Sports Personality of the Year for the second year running.

'Rory had a wonderful year, and my hat is off to him,' Tiger Woods wrote in his 2012 year-end blog. 'He deserved Player of the Year. We'll look at the results in the next five or ten years and see if it becomes a rivalry or not. We'll have to win big events and play each other down the stretch. That hasn't happened yet. We need a lot more of those type of battles, but in bigger events.' As Rory's future unfolds, the legendary rivalry continues to enthral.

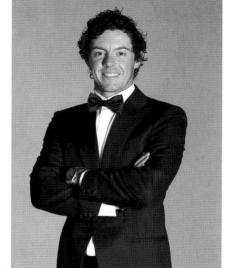

Rory before the Ryder Cup gala dinner celebrations: 'I didn't want the year to tail off. I just wanted to end it in real style.'

ROSS KINNAIRD/GETTY IMAGES

ry looks at his ball during the fourth round of
 DP World Tour Championship, Dubai on 25
vember 2012. The European Tour's finest
 verged on the Greg Norman-designed Earth
 urse at Jumeirah Golf Estates in Dubai, aiming to
 vent a Rory McIlroy sweep at the season-ending
 million (£5.2 million) championship.

M SAHIB/AFP/GETTY IMAGES

Golf is the hardest game in the world. There is no way you can ever get it. Just when you think you do, the game jumps up and puts you in your place. Ben Crenshaw

As a new year dawned for Rory, it heralded a new period in the evolution of his golfing career, both on and off the fairway. He was still getting to grips with all the changes of 2012 as he teed off in the **Abu Dhabi HSBC Golf Championship (21–24 January 2013)** held at **Abu Dhabi Golf Club,** United Arab Emirates.

Earlier that week, Nike publicly announced that they had signed Rory to a lucrative endorsement contract, joining the company's other major client, Tiger Woods. Now both men were making their 2013 season debuts in Abu Dhabi in a European PGA Tour stop.

Rory and Tiger Woods walk down the tenth fairway during day one of the Abu Dhabi HSBC Golf Championship at Abu Dhabi Golf Club on 17 January 2013.

MATTHEW LEWIS/GETTY IMAGES

Woods won their first duel of the new season on day one, while Rory registered two double bogeys. A score of three over par left him eight shots adrift of joint leaders Jamie Donaldson and Justin Rose. He missed the cut. Reflecting on his loss of form, he stated, 'I just need to work on a couple of things. It's still an experimental period.'

Honda Classic, 28 February–3 March 2013
PGA National Resort, Palm Beach Gardens, Florida

Of course, the game is a daily work in progress and it was fair to say Rory was working on new adjustments.

As the year unfolded, Rory's loss of form continued. There were more worries when he unexpectedly walked off the golf course, withdrawing from the **Honda Classic** after hitting his second shot into the water on the par-five eighteenth hole.

Rory walks off the course on the eighteenth hole, his ninth, during the second round of the Honda Classic in Palm Beach Gardens, Florida on 1 March 2013.
STUART FRANKLIN/GETTY IMAGES

The defending champion, who started on the tenth hole, was seven over par after making a double bogey on the eleventh, a bogey on the thirteenth, a triple on the sixteenth and another bogey on the seventeenth. Rory walked straight to his car and left the **Champion Course** at **PGA National Golf Club**.

'I sincerely apologise to the **Honda Classic** and PGA Tour for my sudden withdrawal,' Rory said in a statement later released by the Tour. 'I have been suffering with a sore wisdom tooth, which is due to come out in the near future. It began bothering me again last night, so I relieved it with Advil. It was very painful again this morning, and I was simply unable to concentrate.'

Rory also tweeted this, after he left the course: 'Apologies to all at the Honda. A tough day made impossible by severe tooth pain. Was desperate to defend title but couldn't play on. Gutted.'

Rory was heavily criticised for his withdrawal. Critics claimed that tooth pain was not the real issue. Speculation was rife that Rory was having difficulty adjusting to new equipment.

As the season progressed, Rory insisted the equipment was not the cause of his dip in form.

Despite just making the cut with a shot to spare, his closing round of 66, finishing 12 under par, earned him a superb second place at the Valero Texas Open (4–7 April) in San Antonio. It reduced the number of doubters considerably. Unusually, he opted to play the tournament in preparation for the Masters Tournament in Augusta the following week. He also put his plans to pay a second visit to Haiti with UNICEF Ireland on hold, citing a change in his playing commitments. Rory was keen to concentrate on improving his form.

Later, talking to the *Irish Examiner* on 10 April, he answered a few of his critics, who were unsure of his recent management choices, saying, 'I'm very comfortable and I'm 100 per cent there. I wanted to do it all at the start of the year. I didn't want to leave it for a while and say, "Okay, I'll put something in in dribs and drabs." I just wanted to get it all in, get it all settled and have it over and done with, so eight, nine months down the line, I don't have to say, "Okay, right, I need to try to get this in or that in." It's definitely not the clubs, that's for sure. That's what I've found out over the past few weeks. It's more me.'

A tired-looking Rory speaks to the media ahead of the US Masters.
MIKE EHRMANN/GETTY IMAGES

As Rory looked ahead to his first majors of the year, it was Tiger Woods who claimed more headlines than he did, as the four-time **Masters Tournament** champion returned to the top of the world rankings after three tournament wins. The resurgent Tiger and the heir apparent were yet again being pitched in a duel at the forthcoming **Masters Tournament**.

All the signs were positive, but Rory's wavering form kept him out of the hunt on the final two days. He finished two over par and in a tie for twenty-fifth place. Tiger finished five under par, tying for fourth place. Victory went to Adam Scott.

Rory went on to play the **Wells Fargo Championship** on 2–5 May at **Quail Hollow Club**, where he had stormed to an incredible victory back in 2010. This year he finished in tenth place.

He competed in the **Players Championship** at **TPC Sawgrass**, Ponte Vedra Beach, Florida, on 9–12 May, hoping it would be a great tune-up for the **US Open Championship**. But he tied for eighth place while Tiger Woods raced ahead, victorious, with 15 under par. So far, Rory's form was proving difficult to predict.

At the **BMW PGA Championship** on 23–26 May, held at **Wentworth Club**, Surrey, England, Rory missed the cut.

Rory ahead of the BMW PGA Championship at Wentworth Club, Surrey on 21 May 2013
WARREN LITTLE/GETTY IMAGES

Golf is assuredly a mystifying game. It would seem that if a person has hit a golf ball correctly a thousand times, he should be able to duplicate the performance at will. But such is certainly not the case. Bobby Jones

US Open Championship, 13–16 June 2013
Merion Golf Club, Ardmore, Pennsylvania

Rory's next event was the **Memorial Tournament**. It took place at **Muirfield Village Golf Club, Dublin, Ohio**, between 30 May and 2 June 2013. Matt Kuchar won after finishing two shots clear of his fellow American Kevin Chappell. Tiger Woods finished at eight over par, with Rory struggling at six over par.

This was the sixth **US Open Championship** to be held at **Merion Golf Club** and the first since 1981. Heading an impressive field was Tiger Woods, who, having played in seven tournaments in 2013, had won four. Thanks to the first three of those early tour wins, he had regained his number-one ranking over Rory. Nonetheless, Rory had shattered records on his way to his first **US Open** victory in 2011 and was still deemed a strong contender. Surprisingly, golf's dream duo finished a combined +17 through 54 holes.

En route to a closing score of 76, finishing 14 over, Rory threw a club and buckled another. He had lost his second shot in the creek that protects the eleventh green. He took a drop, but then sent another ball into the same creek. At that, he pushed the Nike club into the ground, completely twisting its head. Rory later tweeted: 'A lot of comments about my bent 9 iron ... moment of frustration and silly thing to do. That's what Merion can do to you!'

Victory went to Justin Rose, who clinched his maiden major title to become the first Englishman for 43 years to win the **US Open Championship**.

Rory throws his club after chipping to the fourth green during the final round of the 113th US Open Championship at Merion Golf Club on 16 June 2013.
ROB CARR/GETTY IMAGES

A long shadow is cast over Rory's performance as he walks off the eighteenth tee during the second round of the 142nd Open Championship at Muirfield, Scotland on 19 July 2013.
RICHARD HEATHCOTE/R&A VIA GETTY IMAGES

Irish Open, 27–30 June 2013
Carton House Golf Club, Maynooth, County Kildare

At the **Irish Open**, Rory's home championship, there was a real sense of anticipation. Rory started his second round well, with a birdie on the first. However, he made five bogeys and only four more birdies, to finish his round on level par and remain on two over for the tournament. Clearly, it was not enough to make the cut.

Now midway through the season, Rory's evident lack of form was generating rumours about his new equipment and the recent management changes.

At the 142nd **Open Championship**, held at **Muirfield**, East Lothian, Scotland (18–21 July 2013), Rory failed to find his form and missed the cut yet again. Just a week after winning the 2013 **Scottish Open**, victory went to Phil Mickelson, who shot a magnificent final round of five-under-par 66, to triumph by three shots.

The 2013 PGA season was not being kind to Rory, who had yet to win a tournament. After his poor round of 78 at Muirfield he confessed, 'I'm trying to focus and trying to concentrate, but I really can't fathom it at the minute. It is a very alien feeling, something I've never felt before.'

Sir Nick Faldo and Jack Nicklaus both offered words of advice, which the press and commentators deemed negative. Rory responded to Faldo's guidance, stating, 'I know he wasn't trying to get on my case, he was just offering words of advice, but I think he has to remember how hard this game can be ... Sooner or later it will turn around and I'll play the golf that everyone knows I am capable of and the golf that I know is capable of winning major championships.'

Rory was right to remain positive and focus on his ability to turn his game around. At the **8–11 August PGA Championship** held at **Oak Hill Golf Club, Rochester, New York** where he tied for eighth place. Rory's belief in his game was at last paying dividends with good results in the wake of what was a difficult season.

Looking ahead

As his career unfolds there will undoubtedly be many more difficulties to overcome and thrilling record-breaking victories to celebrate. What remains fascinating about this journey is Rory's ability to evolve with the game, connect with fellow players on the international circuit and motivate himself to perform above and beyond expectations wherever he steps onto a golf course.

Rory is part of a golfing fraternity that has taken him to destinations across the world. Having honed his skills on spectacular courses across Ireland as a young golfer, Rory still continues to play in Ireland and enjoy some of the most dramatic landscapes in the world.

Christie O'Connor, watched by Ronnie Shade, driving off at Cork Golf Club in 1969
CORK GOLF CLUB

On the banks of Lough Mahon lies Cork Golf Club, which celebrated 125 years in 2013.
CORK GOLF CLUB

History

Many early clubs imported Scottish professionals to teach the game to its Irish enthusiasts. It came into its own in Ireland in the last two decades of the nineteenth century. The first Irish golf clubs were founded in the 1880s, mainly in Ulster and the Dublin area. In the early 1880s, a few holes were laid out in Phoenix Park, Dublin. In 1888, **Cork Golf Club** became the first club set up in the province of Munster. Golf arrived in Connacht in 1894 when a club was established at Rosses Point, Sligo.

The **Irish Amateur Open** was first played in 1892, while the **Irish Ladies Championship** came into being just two years later. The 1890s, turned out to be a boom-time for golf. During that decade golf clubs sprouted all over the country. As early as 1900 Ireland had a dedicated golf magazine, *The Irish Golfer*, whose pages chronicled the exploits of early golfing enthusiasts. By 1901, there were an estimated 12,000 golfers in Ireland.

Daniel Mulhall, History of Ireland.com

in action
ng the pro-
or the 2012
Open, held
e Dunluce
at Royal
ush Golf
Northern
nd on 27

CANNON/GETTY

The growth of railways and the popularity of the bicycle also aided the spread of golf across Ireland particularly in the North. The Belfast and Northern Counties Railway was instrumental the development of golf at Portrush, where the stationmaster would often hold back the Belfast train to accommodate returning golfers.

Daniel Mulhall, History of Ireland.com

County Sligo Golf Course, Rosses Point, flanked by the Atlantic Ocean, with Benbulben as a backdrop
COUNTY SLIGO GOLF CLUB

Of course, Scotland is arguably the home of golf. Rory has played many major tournaments there, including the 139th **Open Championship** at the **Old Course Hotel, Resort and Spa, St Andrews,** Fife (15–18 July 2010), where he tied for third place.

Rory hits his tee shot on the eighteenth hole during the third round of the 139th Open Championship on the Old Course, St Andrews, Scotland on 17 July 2010.
HARRY HOW/GETTY IMAGES

Rory also enjoyed early **Ryder Cup** success on 29 September 2010 at the **Celtic Manor Resort**, Newport, Wales.

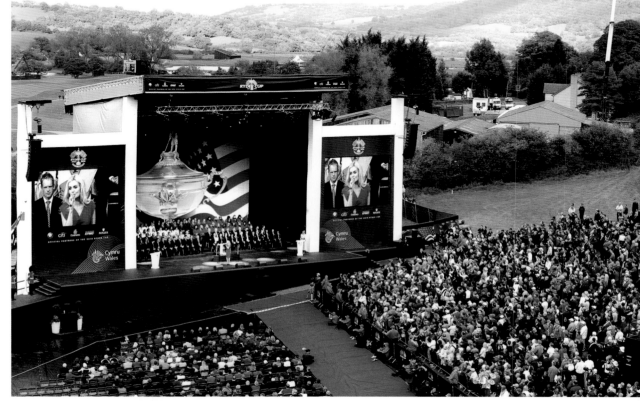

Welsh singer Katherine Jenkins entertains the audience during the opening ceremony at Celtic Manor Resort in Newport, Wales on 30 September 2010.
TIMOTHY A. CLARY/AFP/GETTY IMAGES

Rory tees off on the first hole during the final round of the BMW PGA Championship at Wentworth Club, Surrey on 24 May 2009.
WARREN LITTLE/GETTY IMAGES

It was early days for Rory in his professional career, but his form had been unforgettable as he finished fifth in the 2009 **BMW PGA Championship** (21–24 May) at the majestic **Wentworth Club**, Surrey, England.

A very young Rory takes on the professionals in the pro-am BMW PGA Championship
ANDREW REDINGTON/GETTY IMAGES

The two major titles Rory has earned to date – the 2011 US Open Championship and the 2012 PGA Championship – were both won on American soil.

USA: Early Golfing History

When golf arrived in America at the end of the nineteenth century, it was an elite sport. Early American golf clubs imported their professionals from Britain. In February 1888, after ordering a set of golf clubs from Tom Morris back at St Andrews, Scotsman John Reid gathered together a small group of friends and set up three holes in a cow pasture in Yonkers, New York – the first recorded golf course in the United States. The group formed the **St Andrews Club of Yonkers**, America's first golf club, in November.

thepeopleshistory.com

By the very end of the 1800s, the popularity of the game led many players to suggest an organising body. In December 1894, delegates from golf clubs in Yonkers, Brookline (Massachusetts), Newport (Rhode Island), Southampton (New York) and Chicago met to form the Amateur Golf Association of the United States, later the US Golf Association (USGA), with Theodore Havemeyer of the Newport club as its first president. Within a year, the association had organised the first national open and amateur championships.

thepeopleshistory.com

Way to Go, Mr President!

The game of golf proved popular with many of America's Presidents including: Franklin D. Roosevelt and John F. Kennedy. 15 of the last 19 presidents have been devotees of the game. The 15 golfing presidents are: William Howard Taft, Herbert Hoover, Franklin D. Roosevelt, Harry S. Truman, Dwight D. Eisenhower, John F. Kennedy, Lyndon B. Johnson, Richard Nixon, Gerald Ford, Jimmy Carter, Ronald Reagan, George H.W. Bush, Bill Clinton, George W. Bush and Barack Obama.

thepeopleshistory.com

I would like to deny all allegations by Bob Hope that, during my last game of golf, I hit an eagle, a birdie, an elk and a moose.

Gerald Ford, US president, 1974–77

As a member of the **Ryder Cup** team representing Europe against the United States, Rory has enjoyed enormous success with his European compatriots. The 2012 tournament had a thrilling finish.

The European team poses for a group photo at Medinah Country Club in Medinah, Illinois, on 25 September 2012, ahead of the thirty-ninth Ryder Cup: (top left–right) Sergio García of Spain, Martin Kaymer of Germany, Lee Westwood of England, Peter Hanson of Sweden, Ian Poulter of England, Justin Rose of England, Nicolas Colsaerts of Belgium, Paul Lawrie of Scotland; (bottom left–right) Rory McIlroy of Northern Ireland, Luke Donald of England, José María Olazábal of Spain, Graeme McDowell of Northern Ireland and Francesco Molinari of Italy.
JIM WATSON/AFP/GETTYIMAGES

Playing in Europe, Rory has enjoyed some great successes and spectacular locations during both the professional and amateur stages of his career.

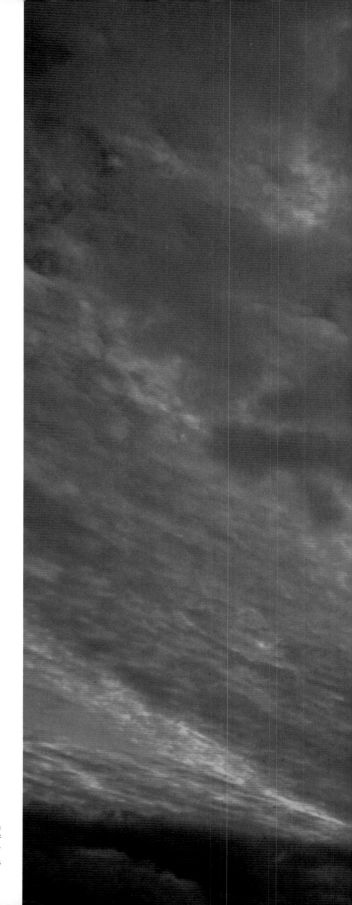

Seventeen-year-old Rory at the Estoril Open de Portugal at the Quinta da Marinha Golf Course in Cascais, Portugal, on 30 March 2007
STUART FRANKLIN/GETTY IMAGES

Golf's precise origins also continue to be something of an enigma. A golf-like game is recorded as taking place as early as 1297 in what is now the Netherlands. There are also earlier accounts of a similar pastime emanating from elsewhere in continental Europe and, even further back, in ancient China.

According to Ling Hongling, Professor of Physical Education, at Northwest Normal University, Lanzhou, P.R. China, the earliest historical record of this golfing precursor was *chuiwan* (*chui* means 'hitting' and *wan* means 'small ball' in Chinese), dating back to AD 943, in records written by Wei Tai of the Song Dynasty. Ling claims that *chuiwan* predates the advent of golf in both the Netherlands and Scotland. Theoretically, he believes it was the Mongolians who brought it to Europe in the twelfth or thirteenth century. Although its exact origins are still to be pinpointed, the twenty-first-century game is thriving in China, Hong Kong and Malaysia.

In 2011, **Lake Malaren Golf Club**, Shanghai launched the inaugural **Lake Malaren Shanghai Masters** tournament. To create a leading international golf event in China, the organisers offered US $5 million of prize money with a US $2 million purse for the champion. The unprecedented prosperity of the event drew the attention of the golfing world, taking the club's status to new heights. In addition to eight Chinese players, organisers invited top international and domestic players, including Lee Westwood and 2011 **US Open Championship** winner Rory.

In the final stages of the tournament, Rory dramatically gave up an early three-shot lead before rallying on the back nine to finish level with USA's Anthony Kim (ranked eighty-second at the time) at 18 under. In a dazzling playoff, Rory went on to win the competition and claim the richest reward in golf.

In 2012, the field was expanded to 78 players and the purse increased to US $7 million. It became a registered European Tour event and was renamed the **BMW Masters**.

The first winner of the **BMW Masters** was Sweden's Peter Hanson, who survived a late challenge from Rory to finish ahead of a supremely talented field with a score of –21.

Today, China is firmly on the global golfing map as a prestigious destination for golfing professionals and amateurs alike, with clubs springing up across the country to meet the increasing popularity of the game.

In 1989 the European Tour Committee expanded into the Middle East with the **Dubai Desert Classic**. Twenty years on, when the season finale moved to the **Earth Course** at **Jumeirah Golf Estates**, the European Tour renamed its 'Order of Merit' the 'Race to Dubai', to reflect these changes.

Today, with tournaments in Abu Dhabi, Qatar and Dubai, the Middle East is a golfing mecca where players of all levels and professionals like Rory, can enjoy world-class championship courses.

ABOVE: Jumeirah's global brand ambassador Rory hits his spectacular final shots of 2011 on the helipad at the Burj Al Arab Hotel, Dubai on 12 December 2011.
DAVID CANNON/GETTY IMAGES FOR JUMEIRAH

LEFT: Rory, enjoying life as a Jumeirah ambassador, hits a shot on a beach in front of the iconic Burj Al Arab Hotel, Dubai before the Dubai Desert Classic on 21 January 2008
DAVID CANNON/GETTY IMAGES

He's going to be the player that kids look up to, that kids measure their own wannabe games by. Graeme McDowell

On show in the Holywood clubhouse is a display room with collections of trophies and memorabilia documenting Rory's career to date. Standing head and shoulders above the array of trophies in the club's display is a replica of his **US Open Championship** trophy along with two of Rory's golf bags – one from the 2010 **Ryder Cup** and another, which he used at the outset of his professional career.

The collection includes his **Royal Portrush Golf Club** record-breaking scorecard of 61, a handwritten thank-you note he sent to club officials, and the MBE medal Queen Elizabeth II presented to Rory following his command performance at **Congressional Country Club**.

Pride of place is a billboard-size photograph of Rory holding the **US Open Championship** trophy, with the large caption, 'Welcome to Holywood Golf Club, home of Rory McIlroy.'

The Rory McIlroy Classic at Holywood Golf Club, 19 August 2011: Ross Nelson with Rory
DARREN KIDD/PRESSEYE.COM

The Next Generation

The club continues to nurture its programme for junior players. Many, just like Rory, have been fortunate enough to experience the mentoring skills of Michael Bannon and thereafter Paul Gray, one of the club's most experienced and highly respected teaching professionals. Holywood Golf Club now has around 180 juniors.

The Rory McIlroy Classic at Holywood Golf Club, 19 August 2011: Rory with Holywood Golf Club ladies' captain, 2011, Sheila Lavery
DARREN KIDD/PRESSEYE.COM

Rory would always come out and play for us, regardless of how busy his schedule might be. He would turn up here to take part in the Senior Cup team events I organised when he was 14, 15, 16 years old and even beyond. Rory would always try to get back here, even though he didn't need to at that stage. But he did because he respected the club and his team players. It's good having him from Northern Ireland and it's an honour to know him. Rory still remembers where he came from. Michael Eaton, HGC captain, March 2012–March 2013

Holywood's had a pretty good history of producing good players. Hopefully, being from here might inspire a few others coming up. Hopefully what I'm doing for the club today can benefit them in some way and help them become better players.

Rory

Rory has become a flag-bearer for the next generation – a truly international hero, someone young people can relate to and follow. He remains an inspiration to people everywhere. Above all, he is a credit to his hard-working family.

On the streets of Belfast he is a hero, and a mural was painted in honour of his achievements. It reflects a very modern hero for our changing times.

The idea for the painting was hatched in early 2012, after Rory was awarded an honorary degree from the University of Ulster. Local artist Danny Devenny was commissioned to paint the mural in Belfast's Holyland area as part of a plan to revitalise and improve the area's image.

A mural dedicated to Rory's success painted on a gable wall in Rugby Avenue in the university area of Belfast
PACEMAKER PRESS

The Rory McIlroy Classic at Holywood Golf Club: Rory makes a presentation to his uncle, Colm McIlroy
DARREN KIDD/PRESSEYE.COM

The **Rory McIlroy Classic** at Holywood Golf Club was initiated to raise money for the junior club. Rory attended the open day to present prizes. After Rory won at **Congressional Country Club**, his father Gerry said to him, 'I suppose you're big-time now and you're not going to be coming to present my prizes?' Rory replied, 'No, no, I'll be there.'

Aerial view of
Holywood Golf Club
SCENIC IRELAND

Holywood Golf Club

Walk the historic fairways of Rory's club

Facing outwards into the mouth of Belfast Lough and the Irish Sea, playing Holywood Golf Course is an exhilarating experience. Many visitors have felt a particular tingle of excitement knowing this is where Rory honed his golfing skills over many years.

When top golfing journalist Bernard McGuire visited the course he described it as, 'Rory McIlroy's Holy Grail' and offered a personal insight of his experience on the course:

'Holywood's opening nine holes, with the exception of the short par three sixth hole, are laid out to the west of the clubhouse. The sixth is named 'Nun's Walk' as you have to cross the roadway to play this downhill 124-yard par three challenge before you then cross back over the road to tackle the lone par five, the 496-yard seventh.

A feature of the seventh is a meandering five-foot wide burn that crosses the fairway about 150-yards out from the green and runs through trees to in front of the eighth tee but then cuts back again crossing the seventh just short of the green.

The challenge at the eighth is to avoid out-of-bounds all down the right side thus placing an emphasis on driving on this dog-left right-to-left 456-yard challenge.

The short ninth hole is an uphill par three that brings you back to the clubhouse and with the 10th, the fourth and last of the par threes, also an uphill challenge...

The 11th, where there is also a burn just short of the green, and 12th holes are laid out at the highest part of the golf course and where you first get to enjoy the full spectacular views out over Belfast Lough. And the further you walk down these two holes the better the view gets'.

Don'ts for Golfers

'Don't miss the beauties of Nature by becoming too absorbed in this game. It will add greatly to your pleasure and improve your play if occasionally you rest your eyes on the landscape.'

Sandy Green, *Don'ts for Golfers*, 1926

The seventeenth hole, Holywood Golf Club
DERMOTT DUNBAR

'The remaining six holes at Holywood run side by side with the 14th, named Quarry, providing the challenge of having to drive your ball from an elevated tee to a tight tree-lined left-to-right dogleg hole before hitting into a sloping green guarded by a left front bunker.

The 17th brings to you back to the clubhouse but there much challenge ahead hitting from a raised tee, and with the clubhouse at your back, the goal at the penultimate hole is to avoid the burn running just in front of the green. Now in standing on the tee of the 394-yard final hole I wondered how many times Rory McIlroy must have stood here being one hole away from winning yet another medal round.

The tee shot is over a ridge to an unsighted fairway below, and with all the trouble down the right side. After playing your second shot remember to ring the 1904 dated bell to let those behind know the fairway is clear.

The green slopes away on the back right corner while there's a bunker front right and a small bunker middle left to catch any errant shots.

Holywood Golf Club is a most enjoyable experience and while playing to a par 69 it's very much a decent challenge. Also like many golf courses in Ireland, the views over out Belfast Lough are so good to take your mind off the golf no matter how well or how poorly you may be playing.

But the greatest reward of all was the pleasure of walking the fairways where such an affable and unassuming U.S. Open champion and PGA Championship winner first honed his golfing skills'.

Source: Bernard McGuire is Freelance journalist European & PGA Tour. Assistant Secretary, Association of Golf Writers. His review article can be read in full on his website www.golfbytourmiss.com

Don'ts for Golfers

'Don't think of the difficulties that beset you either side of the fairway and of the bunkers that yawn between the tee and the green. Make up your mind that so long as you keep your head still and your eye on the ball, there is nothing to hinder a straight shot that will not be penalised.'

Sandy Green, *Don'ts for Golfers*, 1926

he seventh hole
eaturing the five-foot-
vide burn

ERMOTT DUNBAR

Rory's Club is a tribute to our history and Northern Ireland's passion for the game of golf. With a wealth of golfing talent concentrated in our small province, Rory McIlroy has proved himself to be one of our finest ambassadors. His relationship with Holywood Golf Club remains enduring and loyal. It inspires many to come and visit us from all corners of the world. No doubt this will continue as his exciting career unfolds. His work with our younger members and with children around the world reminds us of all of the importance of a shining light and positive influence in our lives who can inspire us all to a brighter future.

Golf is a game that now transcends class, gender and generations. It promotes an inclusive spirit and encourages us all to enjoy its challenges and success every time we step onto the greens, fairways or driving range. We hope you also enjoy the history and legacy of Rory's club.

Paul Gray, general manager, Holywood Golf Club

Aerial view of Holywood
Golf Course
SCENIC IRELAND

This book could not have been prepared and published without the endorsement of Rory's parents together with the support of Holywood Golf Club's team and members.

We are particularly indebted to Rosie and Gerry McIlroy, who have provided us with hitherto unpublished private family photographs of Rory. We wish to thank Gerry for his fascinating insights into his son's early years in Holywood and his unfolding golfing career.

Also, we are very grateful to Paul Gray, Ricky McCormick, Michael Eaton, and Rory's extended family and friends for their invaluable editorial assistance.

Finally, a very special word of thanks goes to Unicef and Golf Clubs across the island of Ireland, the UK and internationally for their personal testimonials and the superb photography they have shared with us.

Rory McIlroy of Northern Ireland tees off at the eighteenth hole during the first round of the Portugal Masters at Oceânico Victoria Golf Club in Vilamoura, Portugal, on 18 October 2007.
RICHARD HEATHCOTE/GETTY IMAGES

Published by Booklink,
Publishing trade name of Cadolux Ltd
www.booklink.ie
Publisher: Dr Claude Costecalde
Published in collaboration with
Holywood Golf Club
www.holywoodgolfclub.co.uk
Edited by Claude Costecalde and Christina Captieux
Text & Picture Research, Christina Captieux
Designer and Picture Editor: Wendy Dunbar
© Design, Booklink, 2013
© Photographs, as credited
Printed in Slovenia
ISBN 978-1-906886-53-0